LIFESTYLE BUILDERS

Advance Praise

"Most business owners do whatever they can to cater to the market but forget the most essential piece: to align their work with the life they want. That's exactly what *Lifestyle Builders* will do for you. Read this now and build your business and your life, your way."

- **Mike Michalowicz**, Author of Profit First and Clockwork

"If you're looking for a clear system to follow on your path to entrepreneurial and lifestyle freedom, look no further! *Lifestyle Builders* lays out the blueprint for strategically designing a business that supports the life of your dreams, instead of dictating how you spend your days. It's the much-needed solution to a design flaw most aspiring entrepreneurs overlook, and one that will set you up for true success."

-**Christine McAlister**, bestselling author of
The Income Replacement Formula & founder, Life With Passion

"Tom and Ariana are the real deal and make a great team. If you've ever wanted to go down the path of being an entrepreneur but it seems risky, mythical, or only for the elite, guess again. In *Lifestyle Builders* they put together a 'how to' manual for transforming your life from employee to entrepreneur. You won't be disappointed."

-**Armando Cruz**, author of *The Legacy Code*
& Creator of the R.I.C.H. Man Experience

"Building a business is hard. Raising a family and maintaining relationships is hard. The two together are insane. Luckily *Lifestyle Builders* has the perfect the guide to building your best life *and* business."

-**Jessica Lorimer**, author of *Smart Leaders Sell*, Sales Coach and Founder of The Smart Leaders Sales Society

"Tom & Ariana are two of the finest people, parents, and entrepreneurs we know. They've truly built a lifestyle they love, without playing by the world's rules. Everything you need to build the lifestyle you want can be found in the pages of this book. Read it now, highly recommended!"

- **Shane & Jocelyn Sams**, Hosts of The Flipped Lifestyle Podcast & founders of FlippedLifestyle.com

"Tom and Ariana are a part of an elite (tiny) percentage of entrepreneurs who actually practice what they preach. Their advice is practical, rock solid, and based on their experiences as successful business owners. Not to mention, they are two of my favorite people in this space. I am so glad their knowledge is being put into the world in a big way!

-**Rachel Pedersen**, CMO and Founder of The Viral Touch, CEO and Founder of Social Media United

"As an entrepreneur of ten years, I know how hard it is to take the business creation process and distill it down to just a few steps. But Tom and Ariana have done it. *Lifestyle Builders* is a no-nonsense, smart, practical plan to help you achieve your business (and life) goals! Grab a copy and get ready to learn from a great couple who's already done it."

-**Philip Taylor**, Founder of FinCon

"Today's online business environment and endless options can be overwhelming to say the least. *Lifestyle Builders* and the advice from Tom & Ariana throughout this book help turn the complex into simple actionable advice that will help you get the business and life you want."

-**Mike Young**, author of *Made Over* and Founder of The Makeover Master

"*Lifestyle Builders* is the GPS you need to take your life from where it is now to where you want it to be. Better yet, it makes darned sure your partner is right there with you, all along the way. Determine your ideal destination for both, make a commitment to staying in the driver's seat and trust that *Lifestyle Builders* will get you there, so long as you don't take your foot off the gas."

-**Heather Gray**, Mindset Expert, Choose to Have it All.com

"What I love about Tom and Ariana is that they've figured out a way to balance 3 businesses, 2 kids and 1 huge mission to inspire the next generation of online entrepreneurs; and do it in a way that is true to them and shows regular, everyday families that this life is totally possible if you have the guts to go for it.
We're grateful to have had the chance to get to know them and watch their journey unfold over the last few years and I know they are *just* getting started with *Lifestyle Builders*!"

-**Jill Stanton**, ScrewTheNineToFive.com

"This book is a MUST-READ for everyone who wants to be successful in life and business. I wish I had this book 15 years ago. As a former employee and now business owner, *Lifestyle Builders* would have helped me not make so many mistakes and build my life with intentionality. We entrepreneurs quit our 40-hour a week job to work 80-hours for ourselves and it is easy to let life slip by. This book helps the reader to make life about living a full life with intentionality and purpose."

-**Dustin Heiner**, founder of MasterPassiveIncome.com

"Tom and Ariana's book will provide any entrepreneurial couple with a financial framework for success! If you want to live your life on your own terms having more time for one another and your family, this is the bible to empower you on your journey!"

-**Dorothéa Bozicolona-Volpe**, Principle, Social Espionage

"With Tom and Ariana's passion for both business and family it was only a matter of time before they shared the blueprint that has helped them have the best of both worlds and that's exactly what you get with this book. The blueprint to building your ideal business and designing your ideal lifestyle."

-**Jason Brown**, founder of Power Trades University

"Many people talk about lifestyle freedom but don't have the plan to achieve it. Tom and Ariana walk you step by step through the process of building your business and mastering your finances, with support for aspects that most business books don't cover, like how to build your company with a growing family and mastering your mindset."

-**April Beach**, Host, The SweetLife Entrepreneur Podcast

"No matter what product you want to sell, no matter what market you're in, the most fundamental part of all business is the business part. *Lifestyle Builders* NAILS the behind the scenes mechanics of WHAT you need to do and WHEN to reduce your risk to nail your market and to finally stop struggling so hard. Make your mark, make your money, and make the lifestyle dreams a reality."

-**Dale Hensel**, Entrepreneur & Mentor

LIFESTYLE
BUILDERS

BUILD YOUR BUSINESS,
QUIT YOUR JOB
—AND—
LIVE YOUR IDEAL LIFESTYLE

TOM&ARIANA SYLVESTER

NEW YORK

LONDON • NASHVILLE • MELBOURNE • VANCOUVER

LIFESTYLE BUILDERS

Build Your Business, Quit Your Job, and Live Your Ideal Lifestyle

© 2020 Tom and Ariana Sylvester

Published in New York, New York, by Morgan James Publishing. Morgan James is a trademark of Morgan James, LLC. www.MorganJamesPublishing.com

ISBN 9781642793802 paperback
ISBN 9781642793819 eBook
Library of Congress Control Number: 2018914100

Cover Design by:
Rachel Lopez
www.r2cdesign.com

Interior Design by:
Christopher Kirk
www.GFSstudio.com

Authors Photo by:
Megan Schultz

Morgan James is a proud partner of Habitat for Humanity Peninsula and Greater Williamsburg. Partners in building since 2006.

Get involved today! Visit
MorganJamesPublishing.com/giving-back

For all the Lifestyle Builders out there, past, present and future.

Table of Contents

Section 3: Concept to Cash

Section 4: Setup & Scale Your Systems

Section 5: Quit Your Cubicle

Section 6: Stop Self Sabotage

Foreword

W̶e've all heard the formula for reaching the American dream - go to a good college, get the right degree, find a job with a great company, put in 35 years, get a gold watch and retire. But does that really accomplish anything beyond creating an income? Does that process address the larger issues of passion, purpose and calling? Certainly not for most people in the workplace today. They've seen what happened to Baby Boomers who followed that plan only to reach the end of their working career with a feeling that nothing had been achieved other than receiving a paycheck. Is that the desired end of a life of work?

Or is there more? In *Lifestyle Builders* you'll see the dangers of working toward "security." Tom and Ariana talk about their own early career paths and realizing the math would not work for ever having financial freedom - or the lifestyle they were dreaming of.

Yes, it's been said that "nothing is more damaging to the adventurous spirit within a man than a secure future." Security is not our friend. It's more likely to bury our adventurous spirit and our passion for being fully alive.

In *Lifestyle Builders* you'll see clearly that "most people have two lives; the one they are living and the one that they want to live." And I know the appeal of the traditional life and the temptation to stay on the "safe" path, rather than following our dreams.

I grew up on a farm where there was a very clear plan laid out for me. I would graduate from high school and then join my dad in the family farming operation -

milking cows at 5:30 AM 365 days a year and throwing hay bales in the blistering heat of summer. But those hours out in the fields simply gave me too much time to dream about doing more, having, more, going more and being more. I chose to leave the world of predictability and pursue the adventure of passion, purpose and profits.

In this book you'll discover you too can choose to design your future. You'll walk through the six steps that will move you from Purpose, to Freedom, to Cash and the lifestyle you have been wanting.

This book will help you clarify "what does your ideal lifestyle look like" as the starting point for "what do you want to do." The more you know yourself the more confidence you can have about doing work that fits you. And the more you know about yourself the more you recognize the freedom you have in choosing work that is meaningful, purposeful, and profitable. And it doesn't matter if you are eighteen or sixty-eight —this process can work for you.

You'll find confirmation that purpose and the thrill of adventure are more appealing and exhilarating than security and sameness. A person fully alive will seek autonomy, mastery and purpose over tenure, pensions, and retirement packages.

Recognizing the freedom we have to choose our work also brings with it the responsibility to accept the results of our work. The sense of fulfillment our work brings, the compensation provided, and the assurance that our work is making the world a better place are all ours to choose. And it's not all about business "success." It's learning how business can serve and enrich our lives. No one is trapped in today's workplace. We get to choose.

For many of you, *Lifestyle Builders* will present a process of waking up the dreams, passions, and visions you had as a child. For some of you the mergers, downsizings, firings, forced retirements and other forms of unexpected change in the workplace in the last few years have served as a clarion wake-up call for dreams that have been waiting patiently for rebirth. Maybe you have been given the opportunity to take a fresh look at "Who am I and why am I here?"

Immerse yourself in this book, allow a fresh expression of those deep urgings that you may have been repressed in your desire to be responsible and mature. What you'll find here is not just another book with lofty theories, but actual systems and processes to take you from where you are to where you want to be. The content is clear and concise, and an easy read for the motivated freedom seeker. The moment you realize that meaningful, purposeful, and profitable work really is a possibility, you've already taken an important step toward reawakening the dreams and passions you may have waiting for release and expression. All of a sudden, complacency and "comfortable misery" become intolerable. The idea of putting your dream on the shelf becomes unacceptable.

Not only do you have the opportunity, you have the responsibility to find or create work that will elevate you to your highest calling. Like many others have chosen, you too can experience the thrilling adventure, as *Lifestyle Builders*.

Enjoy the journey!

Dan Miller, author *48 Days to the Work You Love*

Introduction

When you were a kid, what did you want to be when you grew up?
I wanted to be a marine biologist. I had this weird obsession with whales, complete with small life-like figurines that I gave names and would sit and play with on the floor of my room (which was obviously an ocean), and a "whale mobile" hanging from my ceiling. Even had whale sound CDs, pictures I painted in art class of Orcas, the whole nine yards. My family knew my obsession too. I would open whale-themed presents on my birthday, and no one batted an eye; they knew "Ariana was the whale girl."

Did I end up living out my childhood dream and becoming a marine biologist?

Not exactly. At some point, I realized working with whales would require me to be in the ocean, which happens to be a very large place that is home to some big and scary animals. (I was the girl who was afraid to swim in lakes because fish & seaweed would touch my legs in the dark murky water.)

But while my fear of habitable water scared me off of whale care, my passion for animals still burned bright. Instead of marine biology, I shifted to working with animals on land—not veterinary science, but Zoology. After racking up $46,000 in student loans and earning my degree, I found a job at a local animal shelter where I made minimum wage. At this point, my husband Tom and I calculated that I had to work almost 3 weeks out of the month just to cover my student loan payments! Soon after, I realized this career choice may not have been what I ultimately wanted out of life.

Tom didn't have a childhood dream like I did, but he did enjoy spending time exploring the woods behind his house, playing soccer, and conquering the latest video game. But after getting mononucleosis in 8th grade and missing a year of school, he taught himself how to program computers (nerd). His eventual degree in computer science added $20,000 to our student debt. Worse yet, when he landed a job as a computer programmer, he quickly became disillusioned at the thought of spending his next 45-plus years working 8-12 hours a day holed up in a tiny cubicle.

For us, what we thought we wanted ended up not being what we *actually* wanted. Unfortunately, we were already in $66,000 of debt before figuring this out.

Sure, some people have childhood passions that become their dream adulthood careers and love it, but for many others (like Tom and me), we either abandon our dreams or, once we get there, realize that we want something else. Unfortunately, this is the point when many people give up on going after the life that they want, and instead settle for the path that they are on and the life that they have. After all, it's not easy to change course once you've dedicated so much time and money into a specific career.

Why is this?

Maybe your parents told you that following your dream wasn't realistic.

Maybe you were told that you needed to go to college and pick a career (a lot of pressure to put on an 18-year-old).

Maybe you tried and you weren't able to make enough money to support your dream life, so you settled for getting a job that would pay the bills.

Maybe you were afraid to step out and do something that seems "crazy."

Or maybe you didn't know the path to get there.

Whatever the reasons, most of us got to a point where we decided to stick with the traditional path, the *safe* path, instead of going after our dreams.

What is this *safe* path you may ask? Well, here's what we're told by society:

Step 1: You graduate from high school.

Step 2: You graduate from college.

Step 3: You get a job.

Step 4: You work for 45 years (or more).

Step 5: You fit in life and family around your ever-demanding job.

Step 6: At 65 you can retire (hopefully) and enjoy life.

This is the path that most of us are on, but often it does not lead to the lifestyle that most of us desire. Tom wanted to avoid this path. It scared the hell out of him. And although he had followed it through college, his first job reinforced his fears.

You see, we met the first day of college. Four years later, I was ready to graduate and continue our life together. I was completely content with society's traditional path. Tom, on the other hand, started to come to the realization that the lifestyle that he wanted us to live was not going to come from that traditional path. He could not articulate what his ideal journey was to me, he just knew he didn't like the idea of sitting behind a desk for 45 years. So he did something that I considered crazy at the time: he set a goal to have us both retired by the time we turned 35. That was only 14 years away. He didn't know how it would happen, but that didn't matter to him. As I would come to find out many times in our life, once Tom sets a goal, he sets out to make it a reality.

What we discovered over the course of working towards retirement at 35 was that there are a handful of key activities that set people who build their ideal lifestyle apart from those who do not. On this 10+ year journey (As of the writing of this book we have officially achieved financial freedom, both left our jobs, and turn 35 this year) we learned, implemented and refined these processes. Along the way other people started to take notice and ask us to show them this *secret* process that we created.

Given that it isn't really a secret, we decided to start showing others the process, The Lifestyle Builders Framework. After all, we realized that we had 2 main missions:

- Create the life that we desired for our own family
- To help as many other people as we could to create their ideal lifestyle

Since then, through coaching, online training, workshops, and seminars, we've taught thousands of people—starting in the US and expanding across the globe—this simple process. And today, we want to teach it to you so that you can start building the ideal lifestyle for you and your family.

How This Book is Organized

This book is divided into six major sections, with each section focused in on one piece of the frame work. These are the most important elements in building your ideal lifestyle.

Section 1: "Plan With Purpose." The first step to shift towards the life that you want to live is to define what that life looks like and build yourself a roadmap that directs you from where you are to where you want to be. In this section you'll learn how to identify what your ideal lifestyle looks like and build that initial roadmap for how to get there.

Section 2: "Find Your Freedom." With clarity around your ideal life and a roadmap in place, it's now time to determine what you need to make that happen. You will go through and define your *Freedom Number.* The amount of money and income that you need to leave your job. This includes gathering and understanding all of your financial information, from how much you make, to how much you spend, to how much debt you have, and how much money your business provides you. The goal of this section is to help you get your personal finances in order, as well as help you model your business to achieve your goals.

Section 3: "Concept to Cash." Once you know what it looks like you achieve financial freedom, your next course of action is to create a business that will enable you to achieve it. Most people go about this process by creating the product or service first, then attempting to sell it, but often struggling. This section of the book will show you a better way, focusing on testing and validating your idea to make sure people will pay you for it *before* you even build it. After finishing this section, you'll have a step-by-step process that will take you from creating your idea all the way through making money from it.

Section 4: "Setup & Scale Your Systems." With your business model increasingly becoming more validated, starting with your initial set of sales and continuing with each subsequent sale, you will now shift into designing and organizing your business so that it can continue to grow and drive closer and closer to your goals. In this section you'll learn how to run a business and how to structure and organize it for effective and efficient growth that doesn't take over your life.

Section 5: "Quit Your Cubicle." With a lot of hard work, some pivots along the way, and a little bit of luck, your business will grow to a point where you achieve your Freedom Number and can leave your job. This is an awesome time in your life, but it come with some new shifts and challenges. The goal of this chapter is to help you to make the transition from an employee to a full-time entrepreneur as seamless and possible and help you navigate through some of the obstacles that will arise as you make the transition.

Section 6: "Stop Self Sabotage." How do you make sure you don't get in your own way? Often we are our own worst enemy and inner critic. If you trust the process, you can join the small group of people who not only have big dreams but go after them and make it a reality. The goal of this section is to help you identify the various roadblocks and barriers that will arise and navigate past them so you can put this plan into action.

How to Get the Most Out of This Book

"The only thing you sometimes have control over is perspective. You don't have control over your situation. But you have a choice about how you view it."
Chris Pine, Actor

As Ariana and I were initially discussing the writing of this book, a fundamental question came up: Should we write this book together, or should just one of us write it?

On one hand, we work together in each of our businesses, and obviously in life. People have appreciated this fact and said that they get so much more value because they get both of our perspectives. I am the "natural entrepreneur," with a very visionary and business-oriented mind that is open to explore a new path, while Ariana is the "non-entrepreneur," used to getting a paycheck every two weeks, not worried about how we would pay for health insurance, and not being accountable for the success or failure of the business. We called her the official "reality checker" as she often brought up important concerns early on in our journey (and still does now).

On the other hand, we've always found it initially more challenging when we try to team up on a project. First off, we need to be aligned on what the overall vision is for the project. This means rather than me just jumping in and going to town, I need to take some time to slow down, share my vision, listen to Ariana's vision, and ultimately create a joint vision that works for both of us. Then we need define our individual roles on the project and set parameters on how we will collaborate. So generally, it's easier to fly solo on projects, but when working together on projects they almost always come out *better*.

So, after many discussions and just about every one of our friends telling us that we needed to write the book together, we decided to write the book together (cue peer pressure). Right after we made that decision, we then quickly ran into the next issue: How *would* we actually write a book together? Our writing styles and voice are so different/unique, and we each have very different perspectives on the same story/experience. Whose perspective should we use for each of the stories, and how would you, the reader, know whose perspective you were hearing?

After going back and forth on exactly what the format of the book would be, we decided to arrange it into 6 different sections. For each section, we will start it off with a story, which will set the stage for the section and give you a peek into our journey as we went through this process of building our ideal lives. Then we follow it with specific lessons and actions that you can implement to build your ideal life. The only remaining question was how to write it so that we each brought our unique perspective, without confusing you as to who was talking. In the end, we decided that we would each write the intro story in every section from our own perspective, but then co-write the rest of the section. What we hope what you gain through this format is seeing the different perspectives of how we both viewed the same situation that we experienced, followed by actionable steps to help you move forward and put the pieces in place to build your ideal life.

So when you read the first chapter of each section, you will see "**Tom's Take**" and "**Ariana's Take.**" This will indicate whose point of view you are hearing. As you get into subsequent chapters, we have written them together in a single voice.

"If I have seen further than others, it is by standing on the shoulders of giants."
Sir Isaac Newton, Mathematician & Physicist

Prior to graduating from college, I despised reading. Since then, I have read thousands of books. I often tell people that nothing that I do is original; why reinvent the wheel? Instead, what I do is take the amazing concepts and ideas that I have read, learned, and experienced, and distill/organize them into simple frameworks that makes them easier to implement. Think of me as a walking version of cliff-notes who can breakdown and explain how you can use these concepts in your life & business (and save you the time and energy of reading and understanding all the original books!)

People often thank me for taking all of this knowledge and concepts and packaging then in such a way that not only does it look simple, but that people also gain the confidence that they can actually do it. You will notice that throughout this book there are various stories and analogies to help you better understand the concepts.

We meet people all of the time who are probably smarter than us. In fact, some people that we have worked with have flat out told us this.

"Look, I probably know more about this than you do. But the reason I've sought out you guys is to help me take all of this knowledge I have and turn it into results."

You see, having the knowledge is an important first step, but that is just it. It is the first step. The implementation of that knowledge is what ultimately allows us to succeed and achieve our goals.

So, as you read through this, please realize that all of this is built on the work of those who come before us. So why write this book? Because you shouldn't have to read thousands of books in order to build a business and live a great life. We have taken the key principles, lessons, and steps, and put them into a logical framework for you to follow. As often as we can, we cite the specific source of a concept. In some cases, this can be a challenge, as many of these concepts we have picked up over the course of our journey, and we may not remember where we first encountered them. Additionally, when you read thousands of books, you will find that the same concepts and themes are repeated over and over, so it can often be difficult to know where the concept originated from.

In addition, you will encounter various activities throughout the book. These are the same activities that we use with our clients as we take them through this process. As a thank you for purchasing this book, we've compiled the worksheets and templates that we use with our clients into a special Lifestyle Builders Starter Pack. You will see us reference this pack from time to time throughout the book as we go through the various activities. It contains guides, worksheets, and videos to help you implement and get more out of this book. To download this free starter, head over to www.lifestylebuildersbook.com

Section 1:
Plan With Purpose

Section Summary

Most people have 2 lives: the one they *are* living and the one that they *want* to live. The first step to shift towards the life that you *want* to live is to define what that life looks like and build yourself a roadmap that directs you from where you are to where you want to be.

The goal of this section is to help you get super clear on what your ideal lifestyle looks like and to help you build that initial roadmap for how to get there.

Chapter 1.1

What Are We Doing Here?

Tom's Take

"I'm not sure what to even say. We are getting married in 9 months. What were you thinking?"

Those are not exactly the words that you want to hear out of your fiancé's mouth, especially when you are doing everything that you can to build the ideal life that you desire for the two of you.

You see, Ariana and I had met 5 years before on our first day of college. We began dating about a week later. As we graduated from Oswego State University, I looked ahead at the path we were on. It was that traditional path that we described in the introduction of this book.

Graduate from high school. Check.

Graduate from college. Check.

Get a job. In Progress.

Work for 45-plus years. Ugh.

You see, my degree was in computer science. And at that point, my next 45 years looked like sitting in a cubicle, typing on a computer, working long hours, and savoring my weekends (unless I had to work overtime) before having to repeat the process the next week.

Did you know that 45 years is composed of 2,340 weeks? That's *a lot* of time, and I didn't want to waste it sitting in a cubicle, not enjoying life to its fullest.

You see, I was 21. Forty-five years was more than DOUBLE the amount of time that I had even been alive.

Things didn't look as bleak for her, or so the story in my head went. She had a zoology degree. Her next 45 years could be spent playing with animals and traveling to exotic locations to do so. But while she was doing this, there I would be, stuck in my cubicle. I would miss all of these adventures while she had the time of her life.

Also, not to mention all of the times I would miss in our future kids' lives when they had sporting events or dance recitals or spelling bee competitions. You know the story all-too-well from movies: The father promises to be there but gets stuck at the office working on a project. He keeps looking at his watch and *finally* finishes, rushing out of the office to get to the event. But when he shows up, everyone is gone. He missed it. And his child is devastated.

This was NOT the future that I desired for us and our family.

So I did something crazy, as Ariana would say. As we graduated from college, I set a goal: We would be retired by 35. I had no idea how we would get there, but I figured 14 years would give us enough time to figure it out.

I started figuring out how to make that happen. To do so, I looked around at successful people to see if I could follow in their tracks. What were they doing right that others who sit in cubicles for 45-plus years weren't?

I wanted to see what they did to make money and build wealth. The first thing that stood out was investing in the stock market. So, I started there. I bought a bunch of books about the stock market, such as *The Successful Investor: What 80 Million People Need to Know to Invest Profitably and Avoid Big Losses* and *The Intelligent Investor: The Definitive Book on Value Investing.* I began watching YouTube videos by financial strategists who studied the market for years. I even opened some investing accounts. Then I learned 2 important lessons about the stock market: 1) you generally need money to make money, and 2) there was a lot to learn and I didn't have the patience to learn it all.

After stock marketing investing, I next looked to starting a business. I had had several side hustles throughout high school and college, and many successful people owned their own business, such as Robert Kiyosaki and Donald Trump. I investigated opening a franchise business but found out that you often needed to have a specific net worth, as well as several hundred thousand dollars available. So that wasn't going to work. I then checked out some Multi-Level Marketing

(MLM) companies. If you are not familiar, these are the companies that you sell products for, such as health supplements, jewelry, and other similar products. After checking out a few companies, I just didn't get a great vibe from any of them.

So, I went back to the drawing board, and then I found it - real estate investing! It seemed like every wealthy person had real estate investments. Better yet, as I began doing research, I came across this concept of buying a duplex as your first investment property. You live in one half and rent out the other half. If you do it right, you could then live for free, or for very low cost. Given that we were already spending $750 a month to rent a 2-bedroom apartment, this seemed like an awesome opportunity for us. So, I approached Ariana with the idea, all excited, only to get shot down. She wanted us to buy a house for ourselves like we had originally discussed. She wanted nothing to do with being landlords.

I was running out of ideas. Nothing seemed to be working, and Ariana seemed to say no to every opportunity. Demoralized and depressed, I drove home from work one evening questioning whether retirement by 35 could really be done. Then I heard an advertisement come across the radio that changed my life:

"Sick of your job and not living the life that you want? Do you want to learn how to build real wealth and start living your life? Join us for this limited 2-hour free training on how to become a real estate investor!"

This was it. I just needed to learn different ways to invest in real estate so that we wouldn't be landlords.

I went home and signed up. I also got an extra ticket. Clearly Ariana was not going to go with me, so I called up my cousin Kip and convinced him to go. The night of the event came. There were lots of people there, and although they didn't actually show you much about how to invest in real estate, they did do an awesome job of getting you excited for the life that you could create through real estate investing. They offered an additional 3-day training where they would dive deeper into various strategies for only $500. And you could bring a friend, while also getting some audio programs and workbooks to get you started. So Kip and I decided to split the $500 cost and go to the 3-day training.

On the car ride home, I listened to disc one of the audio lessons. That night I tore through the workbooks and was so excited for the training. When it came, there were probably 75 to 100 other people who decided to attend. The training was held on a Friday, Saturday, and Sunday from 7AM - 5PM, so they were long days, but I showed up excited.

The next 3 days were a brain dump of information. They discussed concepts from the audio trainings. They provided an overview of real estate investing and financing your deals. They went into various investment strategies and showed example deals.

On the last day, the next sales pitch started. They passed out sheets of paper with their "advanced" training session. We then each wrote in the "regular" prices and the "discounted" prices if you signed up today. And as I know now but didn't know then, the entire 3 days had been strategically organized to get people to invest in the next set of training at the end.

As I wrote down the prices, I was shocked. The lowest cost training was $5,000 for a single course, and they went all the way up to $45,000, which was more than I made in a year at that point. I knew right away that we were not going to invest in any of these courses.

But then I thought about it (The sales tactics and psychological conditioning from the past 3 days was working). I saw other people sign up. They were praised for taking action and investing in their future. And as I thought about my future, I knew I didn't have enough information to invest in real estate, especially because Ariana wasn't on board. So how was I going to achieve that goal of retiring by 35? If we did invest, it would *only* be $7,500, since I could split the $15,000 with Kip. But I didn't have $7,500, so that wasn't possible. Oh, but I did have a few credit cards with some space. If I did invest, I would be able to make this money back pretty quick, right? Just like the presenter talked about; a single deal could be worth $5,000, $10,000, or more. It would only take 1 or 2 deals, which I could definitely do if I got additional training courses and guidance, right?

I was torn, but in the end, my cousin and I decided to sign up for a package that included 4 additional trainings. I ended up having to split the cost over 2 credit cards. When they processed the transactions and gave us our new materials, I was excited, but also a little sick to my stomach. Ariana and I had just bought a house and were planning to get married in a few months, and I had just added another $7,500 to our debt (which also included $66,000 in college loans, if you recall from earlier), for a training course on real estate investing, which she didn't want us to do anyways. On the bright side, I guess if I didn't make this work, then we wouldn't have to worry about adding on more debt from the wedding, as Ariana would probably call it off…

Ariana's Take

"I'm not sure what to even say. We are getting married in 9 months. What were you thinking?"

Those were the words I said to Tom, after he told me about his latest business venture—a $7,500 investment into 4 real estate trainings. He spent $7,500 we didn't have, on 2 credit cards, without discussing it with me, his fiancé and partner in life. We had just bought a house together 6 months before, spent money on improvements, and we were gearing up to pay for our own wedding with 250 guests in just 9 months.

I had a brief (it felt much longer in my head of course) moment where I wondered if I even knew him anymore. Had he changed so much in the time since we graduated from college that I didn't see this coming? What had possessed him to do something so risky and expensive when we were just starting out our lives together?

We sat in silence in that dark and quiet living room. The only noise that echoed in our house came from the dog shifting close by in her bed and me sniffling into a pile of tissues. The light illuminated the kitchen, creating weird shadows on the wall next to me.

"I guess I just don't understand WHY. How did we get here?"

And that was the crux of it. The end of our first story and the beginning of this new one. The *Why*.

You see, our lives together thus far had been so simple, so easy. Four years of college, deepening our connection and friendship, knowing we'd spend the rest of our lives together. Talking all things life: jobs, marriage, house, kids. "The Path" as it were.

Except somewhere in those couple months in between college and our first jobs, Tom read a book that changed his whole view on life. A friend had given him a copy of *Automatic Millionaire* by David Bach. After reading it, Tom was apparently spending his time thinking about how he could do this and seeing this dream of financial freedom for us and our future family.

One Problem: He *kinda sorta* forgot to share these thoughts and dreams with ME. While I looked forward to the traditional life path, Tom took that flying leap towards his dreams and left me to fall flat on my face.

I felt betrayed and confused. We were best friends. We had spent the last 5 years doing *everything* together—late night snack trips to the dining hall, holidays with our extended families, binge watching *Sopranos* for days, even grocery shopping and laundry. We told each other everything, shared all of our fears, and even revealed, in detail, our most embarrassing moments. So *how did I not see this coming?* Was I that far detached from the man I was supposed to marry? Did I have some serious rose-colored glasses on, clouding what was really going on here?

How DARE he do this to me as our life was just starting to move forward? I had worked hard, graduated from college with honors, successfully played soccer for 4 years, done the internships and stuck by him through all the tough times during college. I had done everything right! I deserved a good life, and a partner who was going to help me find one. Not someone who would go behind my back and do something so *risky*. What in the actual hell was he thinking?!

Hours later, and many tear-soaked tissues (not just mine this time) we came to a better understanding. We hadn't realized how differently we had each been thinking about our future. We both had the same end goal, but our assumed paths to getting there were miles away. That tough conversation allowed us to see the gap and talk through what we each wanted. I now knew WHY he was so desperate to get out of the "rat race" and the path we were currently on. He couldn't bear the thought of sitting, miserable, behind a desk for 45 years. Becoming the resentful, sad husband. He didn't want me aimlessly wandering, unfulfilled, from job to job. His ultimate dream was to create an amazing life for us, and someday for our kids. To be financially set and have the freedom to do what we wanted in life. To do work we loved and not be beholden to jobs and careers that sucked the life out of us.

And lucky for us, those dreams were exactly what I wanted for us too. I just still wasn't sure how we were going to achieve it.

Chapter 1.2

Describe What You Want to Have

What does your ideal lifestyle look like?

That's one of the first questions that we ask most people who approach us about starting a business. Most people look at us confused, or like a deer in headlights.

"Tom, I came to you for help starting a business, why are you asking me about my life?"

or

"You know, Ariana, I'm not really sure. I just know that I feel like I'm currently on a hamster wheel and I want off."

What we often find, and it was true the first time that we asked ourselves this question, is that most of us know that we want more out of life, but often we can't define what "more" really means. We all have this idea of what we want our lives to look like, but it often seems fuzzy and unobtainable, especially if the people who we interact with in our daily lives seem content with their current lives.

Who are you to want more?

Why aren't you more grateful that you have good jobs and can feed your family?

Don't you know there are people who would kill to be in your position and have a secure job that pays what you make a year?

We hear the questions, comments, and criticisms when we share these thoughts with those around us. This is often the point that people stop. They periodically get the inspiration that they could have a better life, but just like crabs

19

in a barrel, the people around them quickly share all the reasons why thoughts like that are ridiculous. And they go back to their life as it currently exists, letting their dreams drift away. This is unfortunate, as often people look back and regret not going after their dreams.

Years ago, Tom had a conversation with a family member (we'll call him Uncle Fred). He talked about our vision, our plan. Fred could not fathom why anyone would walk away from such a well-paying job. He didn't understand why we'd risk leaving that *stable* career to take such a chance on an unknown. To us, we valued our freedom and impact over the money, and knew that we would ultimately be able to make more money as business owners than employees. We were willing to take that risk and believed we could achieve it. Not everyone has the same view, so they often don't go after what they truly want. Yes, there is a risk in going after your dream, but there is also a risk in staying where you are. Which one would you rather take on; one that provides the opportunity to live your ideal life, or one that causes you to always wonder if you would've achieved more? People like Fred prefer the stability of the latter.

But if you are reading this book, you are likely ready for change and are willing to go after what you desire. You realize that there is more for you and your family out there, and you are seeking a path for how to achieve it. So, after you come to the realization that there is a gap between where you are and where you want to be, the next step is getting clear on where you want to be.

When thinking about setting a path for your future, consider it like using a GPS. When you use a GPS, you go through a few simple steps:

Step 1 – Enter your destination

Step 2 – Enter your starting point

Step 3 – The GPS plots out your best path, with a few alternatives one, with some estimated timeframes and checkpoints along the way

Planning out your ideal life is no different. We will start with Step 1, which is defining your destination. Now there are many different activities that you can use to define your destination, but we've narrowed it down to the ones that we find people have the most success with.

Plan Your Life

"Begin With The End In Mind"
Stephen R. Covey

There are only a few books that Tom will consistently read every few years, one of which is *The 7 Habits of Highly Effective People* by Stephen R. Covey. If you ask him, he would say it is the most influential book for how to become a better person and improve your life.

You see, most people drift through life, not being intentional with their thoughts and actions. In *The 7 Habits*, Covey provides a simple framework for leading an effective life. Although every habit is valuable, we'd like to highlight this second habit related to our current topic. This is the habit that Tom references most often, pretty much anytime we decide that we want to do something:

"Begin with the end in mind"

When you begin with the end in mind, you define your destination. This is the first piece of information that your GPS needs. Although it may seem simple, there is much more beneath the surface that you don't realize until you really take some time to consider where it is you want to go. Your destination is composed of multiple elements, so in order to simplify them and allow you to take some action towards improving your clarity, we will break them up into 3 areas:

Purpose

Vision

Ideal Everyday Experience

Before we go too much further, let's first define what we mean by each of these words in the context of achieving your life dream.

Purpose - The idealistic reason that you and your family exist

Vision - The things that you and your family aspire towards

Ideal Everyday Experience - The way you and your family want your typical day to look

You will notice that each definition not only includes you, but also your family. If you are in a relationship, it is important to do this activity with your spouse. Both of you have different backgrounds, and likely different views on not only what sort of future you want to create for your family, but also how you will get there.

This was very evident in the story that opened this section of the book. Both of us had very different perspectives on not only what our future looked like after college, but also the approach that we would take to get there. Had we spent some time going through this activity early on, we would have realized some of these differences and would have had the opportunity to understand each other's expectations and get aligned. Below is a chart to help you and your spouse develop a family plan while considering each other's perspectives.

Sketch of the first page of the Life Planner.
Fillable Template available in the starter pack @ lifestylebuildersbook.com

Purpose

In *The 7 Habits of Highly Effective Families*, a follow-up book where Covey applies the 7 principles to families, he calls this concept co-missioning.

The power of co-missioning is that it literally transcends *your way* and *my way*. It creates a new way, a higher way: *our way*.

As you go through these next activities to clarify and craft what you want your life to look like and fill in your Life Planner, it is critical that you include the key people in your life who will be part of and/or be impacted by what you come up with. If you are not in a relationship, then you will be the core contributor to what you want your life to look like. You may take some input/guidance from those close to you whose opinion you value, but you are in the driver's seat because the destination it what will make *you* happy—and you don't want someone else who doesn't have your goals in mind holding the steering wheel.

If you are parents, you can ask your kids for their input. Obviously, they can contribute more as they grow older, but even starting discussions and asking questions when they are young will spark some really good conversations. Asking questions about how you can be better parents, make their lives fuller, and how they can help contribute to the family unit not only opens up some great dialogue, but it also gets them thinking of these things from an early age setting the foundation for them to grow into a great person.

> **Lifestyle Builder Starter Pack Resource**
> The Life Planner Worksheet will help you organize and define these 3 key areas of getting clarity on your life. This is included with your starter pack that you get for free with this book.
> Get your free copy at www.lifestylebuildersbook.com

Family Mission

You may be rolling your eyes when you see the words "mission," especially because we are talking about your life. So as we did above, let's first define what we mean when we say mission.

Mission - The thing that drives you towards your purpose

Often times businesses will wordsmith a mission and fill it with a bunch of buzz words so that no one really understands what it means, and it could be applied to any business.

For example, see the below mission for a company.

"_____ provides its customers quality office and information technology products, furniture, printing values and the expertise required for making informed buying decisions. We provide our products and services with a dedication to the highest degree of integrity and quality of customer satisfaction, developing long-term professional relationships with employees that develop pride, creating a stable working environment and company spirit."[1]

What does that even mean?

In fact, this is the mission statement for Dunder Mifflin, the fictional company portrayed in the hit TV series "The Office." "The Office" is a satirical look at modern office life, complete with a generic and bland mission statement that could pass for many real-world businesses.

So why would you want to go through this activity as part of planning your life? The answer lies in what a mission statement actually is.

A mission statement should be unique and help define the reason for existing, as well as the specific dynamics. This is what drives you towards your purpose. So when we apply this to your life, this helps you and your family understand what you strive for, what makes you unique, and how you should operate. Doing this will now give context and meaning to everything else that you do.

Family Mission Statement

As mentioned earlier, this concept is from the book *The 7 Habits of Highly Effective Families.*

"A family mission statement is a combined, unified expression from all family members of what your family is all about — what it is you really want to do and be — and the principles you choose to govern your family life."

Although Tom had always learned about vision, mission, culture and other concepts in relation to his job through the lens of business, these concepts are equally if not more powerful when applied to your family. When businesses fail, you can often trace back some root causes of the failure to a lack of mission clarity. It's no different with a family. When a family fails, you can often trace back the different expectations and lack of clarity around some of these key concepts. Neither businesses nor families fail overnight, but typically over years of doing things but not being intentional about their mission. For example, if one spouse wants lots of children and the other would prefer not to have kids.

There are different ways to go about creating a family mission statement, but here is what is proposed in Covey's book and works best in our experience. The goal is to create a single sentence to answer the following questions:

- What is the purpose of our family?
- What is this family about?

In our experience, you do not get this answer in a single sitting—it takes weeks, sometimes months, to get to the core of what this should look like. It helps to write this out in a longer form initially, then over time work on condensing it. Tom often finds that it is easier to write out an entire page—or even multiple pages—and then trim it down. By doing this you allow your family to continue trimming this down until you are left with the most important elements.

> *"I have made this longer than usual*
> *because I have not had time to make it shorter."*
> Blaise Pascal

It can take time to consider varying ideas and condense them down into a single sentence or thought. Many people benefit from noting the answers to various questions, then working to go from multiple pages to a single page, then from a single page to a single paragraph, and then from a single paragraph to a single sentence.

In addition to the two questions above, here are some additional questions to use as a way to think about your family mission statement, and, over time, work to condense it down to one simple, yet meaningful, sentence.

- What kind of marriage/relationship do we want to have?
- What expectations do we have of each other?
- What roles do we each play?
- What kind of family do we really want to be?
- What kind of parents/children do we want to be?
- What kind of people will our children need to be to succeed in the world?
- What do we want to be remembered by?

Consider all the questions above as you begin exploring this, and feel free to add your own questions. Anything that helps you create your best family mission statement will only help guide you on achieving your goals and living your dream life. Remember, this and each of the following activities will help you increase clarity on your ideal life.

In the book, Covey shares their family mission.

To always be kind, respectful, and supportive of each other,

To be honest and open with each other,
To keep a spiritual feeling in the home,
To love each other unconditionally,
To be responsible to live a happy, healthy, and fulfilling life,
To make this house a place we want to come home to.

And here is ours.

To create a happy and purposeful life, filled with amazing experiences
that bring our family closer, and as well as allowing each of us to grow
into the best versions of ourselves to be able to have a positive impact on
others that we care about.

Core Values

Core values are your key beliefs that guide your behavior and help you make decisions. Although there are different definitions of what a core value actually is, we will use a definition from Patrick Lencioni in his book, *The Advantage*:

"Think of your Core Values as a few behavior traits that are inherent in the organization. They lie at the heart of the organization's identity, do not change over time and must already exist. In other words, they cannot be contrived."

Although he was describing core values in the context of a business, this definition also applies very well to our personal lives. So here is the simple definition for us to use:

Core Values - How we behave

You see, we all already have values that are within us. These values guide our decisions and determine how we behave as we navigate through life. Often times we may not be completely aware of them, but by taking some time to understand and define what they are, we can now live more intentionally.

So just like with defining your mission, it can take some time to extract your core values and bring them to the surface. To start the process, ask yourself and your family the following questions:

- What quotes of philosophies guide each of us individually and also collectively as a family unit?
- For major decisions that we've made, what factors led to the final decision?
- What things do we consider when making an important decision?

- If we asked others to describe us and what's important to us, what would they say?

As you go through this activity, it is important to remember that your core values are not created out of thin air but extracted and captured from what you already do. Analyzing your behaviors and decisions can help you define your core values, leading to a better understanding of how to achieve your Ideal Everyday Experience.

As an example, here are the 5 core values that we identified for us.

1. Always Do The Right Thing
2. Your Life. Your Business. Your Way.
3. Walk The Talk (No Sugar Coating)
4. Family First, Then Impact (Family Relationships) - Put your oxygen mask on first
5. Collaboration, Not Competition (Business Relationships)

As you will see, we defined each of these as a short phrase, sometimes with clarification in parenthesis. Each of these phrases means something specific to us. Your core values should be the same. They may be a single word, but what we've often found is by expanding a single word into a short phrase, it allows you to create more specific meaning to you. For example, we could have used "Integrity" instead of "Always Do The Right Thing", but to us, always do the right thing is clearer and more meaningful. Make sure that your core values speak to you. When you finish this activity, read them back and test them out against your behavior and decisions and feel free to refine them if you find any disconnects. For example, after we defined our core values, we tested out "Always Do The Right Thing" by thinking of difficult decisions that we have had to make.

Legacy

Your legacy is how people will remember you when you are gone, as well as the lasting impact that you leave on the world. When you define the legacy that you want to have, you can then create and start living your legacy now instead of waiting until you are gone.

As you go through life, there are two main modes that you will fall into: survive mode and thrive mode.

Survive mode is where many people are stuck. They are just trying to make ends meet. Each day is focused on themselves and their family, working on satisfying their *own* needs—not on the happiness they can achieve by helping others. While in this mode, you often spend very little time thinking about your community and how you can help more with people/causes that you care about. Unfortunately, many people never get out of survive mode because they only focus on short term needs and never take the time to step back and look at the bigger picture.

Thrive mode is when you have yourself and your family covered, *and* you start impacting people beyond yourself in a positive way.

It can be a weird feeling when you start to transition from survive mode to thrive mode, especially as an entrepreneur. You've likely spent years working hard and just trying to make ends meet. You've made sacrifices, have worked hard, navigated past failures, kept going when people said it wouldn't work, and kept at it. Then "suddenly" (more like after years of hard work), you wake up one day and realize that you and your family have everything that they need. You can make more money, but the money itself will not significantly change your life.

Many people get lost at this point. They don't understand how to make the shift from surviving to thriving. What once motivated them, taking care of themselves and their family, has now been accomplished and they now need a new source of meaning and motivation to help drive them forward and make them happy. Additionally, all of these unexpected feelings start coming up, such as questioning if you deserve the success that you have or feeling guilty now that things seem to come to you easier. Sometimes this may be referred to as fear of success. You've been trained to work hard, go against the grain, and take care of yourself. Once you get past that point and figure things out, you almost get lost (ironically). You begin to question yourself.

"Who am I to make all this money?"

"I don't deserve this."

"What if people find out that I'm a fraud?"

"Making more money is greedy."

"What if I lose it all?"

"Maybe I should stop while I'm ahead."

This is a critical spot as an entrepreneur. Many people have sabotaged their success at this point, because they don't know how to make the transition from surviving to thriving. They've worked so hard to make money and, now that they have achieved financial freedom, they don't know what to do next. The stories that they have in their head from childhood and their life experiences begin to come out, and without addressing them and having a bigger purpose, everything can begin to unravel.

This is where thrive mode comes in. The focus goes from internal to external. It goes from helping yourself and your family, to helping others. It goes from deriving value and happiness from helping you to helping others.

If you've ever had the opportunity to speak to people near the end of their lives, you will truly get to experience what legacy means. Quite often as we go through life, we give very little thought to our legacy, but someone who has experienced life and is close to death often has their legacy at the forefront of their thoughts. They are reflecting on their lives, what they did and didn't do, as well how people will remember them.

But why do we need to wait until the end of our lives to have these thoughts? How powerful would it be to have these thoughts much earlier in your life? It would allow you to define how you want people to remember you and live intentionally every day, building a memorable legacy throughout your life. And when you are near the end of your life, you won't have to speak from a place of regret, but from a place of fulfillment in knowing that you made the most of your life and made a positive impact on the lives of others.

A powerful activity that you can use to help you achieve this is to write your own obituary, first as it would be and a second time as you would want it to be. It sounds morbid, I know, but it is such an effective way to get yourself into the mindset of how you want people to remember you. Writing these 2 versions will help you identify the differences between how people view you now vs. how you want them to view you. In doing this activity, you can then clarify the legacy that you want and begin acting in a way that starts creating the legacy today.

As you go through and write this, ask yourself the following questions:

- What does a successful life/family look like?
- What do we want to be known/remember for?

- What words do we want people to associate with us?
- What impact do we want to make?
- What lessons have you learned that you want to be passed down to future generations?

As with each of the subsequent activities, the process and discussion around this topic is often more important than the end results that you write on paper.

And one final tip: Many people will treat survive mode and thrive mode as two distinct phases. During survive mode, they just focus on themselves and their family. Then once their family is taken care of, they then shift into thrive mode. It doesn't have to be this way. You will find a lot of power and value from incorporating elements of thrive mode, even while you are in survive mode.

What does this mean? Here is a common example. While you are working on making more money and taking care of your family on your path to financial freedom and thrive mode, allocate a portion of your resources (time, money, experience) to helping others. This can start with as little as 1%, with increases over time. What you will find is that by doing this, you will be experiencing thrive mode throughout your life, and the transition will be much smoother. Also, you will be living your impact, and be the person you need to achieve thrive mode.

What could this look like?

- If your salary is $50,000/year, donating 1% would mean $500 a year or less than $10 a week. As you make more money, the amount of money that you give automatically increases. Then over time, you can continue increasing your impact by increasing from 1% to 2% and beyond.
- Assuming you work ~40 hours/week, 1% of your work time would be about 20 hours a year or less than 30 minutes a week. You could give this time to help someone or something that you care about.
- If you have a product or service (or a skill), you can donate 1% of that to help a cause that you care about. With a skill, this amplifies that 30 minutes a week mentioned above as it could save the person or cause both time and money.

The key here is looking for small opportunities to start helping others and over time making incremental increases in how much you give.

Culture

What memories do you have from your childhood? What traditions does your family follow? What does your family do that is unique and different than other families?

More often than not, the answers to these questions make up your family culture. For Tom, one tradition was driving around as a family in December and looking at Christmas lights. For Ariana, it was making massive amounts of Christmas cookies using her Grandparent's cut-out recipe with those tiny anise seeds (yum) that they then frosted.

As you become an adult, you will carry some of your family culture with you. If you enter into a relationship with a spouse, they will bring some of their own family culture. And if you decide to have children, your family will likely create its own culture. Culture allow families to build strong relationships and reinforce their core values, creating and supporting the uniqueness of the family. They make the family tighter-knit and provide an identity.

Culture can be passed down from generation to generation, while also morphing and being shaped by each generation. Beyond just being passed down, it often encompasses the previous concepts that we discussed: Purpose, Family Mission Statement, Core Values, and Legacy.

A brief reminder of our definitions:

Purpose: The idealistic reason that you and your family exist.

Mission: The thing that drives you and your family towards your purpose.

Core Values: How you and your family behave.

Legacy: The impact you and your family have and how you will be remembered.

Family culture helps carry on these concepts into the future. They allow us to not only continue on with what we learned and experienced growing up, but also to morph and evolve to make it our own as we move through life.

Culture help define your family. Even though family's cultures can be similar, each family evolves its own culture as no two families have exactly the same traditions, so part of it is your mark. It gives family members something stable to rely on. No matter what ups and downs you experience in life, the traditions can be familiar and act as a grounding point to reinforce your family. This is similar to businesses. Google has a specific culture that is different from Amazon. That culture helps people who are part of it live with the same purpose, mission, core values, and legacy of the company.

To come up with your family's list of traditions, discuss the following questions:

- What memories stand out from each family member's childhood?
- What activities did your family do every year that you loved?
- What "magical moments" existed for each family member in childhood?
- What new traditions do you want to introduce to your family?
- What makes your family culture unique compared to other families?

Traditions make your family unique, and each generation should be unique. Part of capturing your family traditions doesn't just mean reflecting on the past, but also creating the future. So it is also important to decide what traditions you will enhance or add into the mix with your family.

Vision

Your vision is what allows you to look into the future and get clear picture of what you want your future to look like. It gives you something to strive towards. Think of it as your north star, guiding you forward in the right direction.

Not all visions are crystal clear, though, and some can even be abstract. For example, you may say that you want to travel more or live in a bigger house, but it can be tough to wrap your head around what each of those specifically looks like, which then can make it hard to achieve. To solve this issue and make abstract visions turn into specific visions, create a vision board.

There are many different ways to create a vision board, but we like to develop ours using four simple organizational categories:

1. The "Things" you want to have
2. The "Experiences" that you want to have
3. The "Relationships" that you want to have
4. The "Impact" that you want to make

With these defined, you will then be able to model/design the ideal business (in a later chapter) that will enable you to have the above four things. Let's take a look at defining them by exampling each category individually.

Things

Most people have material possessions that they desire. These include things like:

- Living in your dream house
- Driving a vehicle that you love
- Having nice equipment for your favorite hobbies
- Buy the clothing or other items that you desire

Make a list of the things that you would like to have as part of your ideal lifestyle. You will use this list to help create your vision board.

Experiences

In addition to things, many of us desire specific life experiences. Experiences include things like:

- Unforgettable vacations to new and exciting destinations
- Being able to spend time with friends/family
- Creating memories that last you a lifetime
- Milestones, such as being there for your child's first day of school
- Spending time doing hobbies that you enjoy

Make a list of experiences that you want to have as part of your ideal lifestyle. You will use this list to help create your vision board.

Relationships

People are what give most of us true joy in our lives. The people that we surround ourselves with, including the ones who help us, and the ones who we help, such as:

- Your role as a son/daughter
- Your role as a spouse
- Your role as a parent
- Your role as a friend
- Your role in your community
- Your role in various groups and social circles

Make a list of roles that you play/relationships that are important to you. You will use this list to help create your vision board.

Impact

Impact goes beyond us and toward leaving a legacy of helping others. These include things like:
- Creating a better lifestyle for your family/children
- Helping your favorite charity
- Tackling a problem in your community, city or state
- Helping others overcome challenges and achieve more happiness

Make a list of the impacts that you would like to make in other people's lives. You will use this list to help create your vision board.

Business

With the previous 4 categories defined in your ideal lifestyle, now you get the opportunity to describe the type of business that you would like to create, which will enable these opportunities for you. This could include things like:
- A business that brings you home $10,000/month
- A business that helps solve a major problem that you are passionate about
- A business that allows you to work 4 days a week
- A business that gives you the flexibility to make your own schedule

Make a list of these characteristics that describe your ideal business which enables your ideal lifestyle. Note that this is not saying the specific business that you will create (we will get to that later), but that you are simply describing the *characteristics* of the business that you will create.

Now that this is defined, you can physically (or electronically) create your vision board. Find images that represent the items on each of your 4 lists (things, experiences, relationships, and impact) and put them together to create your vision board. Then place this board somewhere where you will see it often to help keep you inspired and focused on what you want as part of your ideal lifestyle.

> *Note: Throughout this book, we will reference owning your own business and being an entrepreneur. This is because we believe that this is one of the best ways to be able to truly create your ideal life. With that said, these principles apply across the board. So if you enjoy your career and don't plan to leave it, realize that you can utilize many of these same principles to design your career.*

For some examples of complete vision boards, head over to lifestylebuilders-book.com. As you go through this, realize that like the previous activities, the process of gaining clarity on your priorities—and your family's priorities—is more important than the end result. With that said, the end result can serve as a source of inspiration as you work towards your continued success.

Some people really enjoy creating a visual board (virtual or physical), complete with pictures that represent and inspire what they want to achieve. This can often act as a strong reminder when you then display it somewhere that you will see it every day.

For others, they may not be as into gluing pictures to a traditional vision board, but that doesn't make this activity any less valuable. Your output may be a simple list of what's important to you in each of these areas.

Just remember that so much of the value in an activity like this is from the journey, not the destination.

Ideal (Every)Day Experience

With some clarity on your ideal lifestyle vision coming from the process of crafting your ideal vision, another useful activity is thinking about what you want your typical day to look like.

Often times people talk about their "ideal day." Perhaps they like sleeping in, only to be woken up by the calming sounds of the ocean's rising tide. Breakfast mimosas replace brunch and laying on the beach with a good book and a year-round tan. This is often defined as your *ultimate day*. And while it sounds fun in theory, the reality is you will likely not be living your ultimate day every day. It is not practical, and to be honest, it would not be as special if you did it every day. Think of it like buying your dream car vs. renting it for a week. If you buy the dream car, eventually you have to change its oil, replace its tires, be leery of parking it and getting scratches—your dream becomes tainted with problems. But if you occasionally rent the car, you get all the joys and fun of it without having to worry about the problems. That's what an ultimate day is more like, which is why making an ultimate day your every day is problematic (you have to worry about hurricanes, running out of mimosa ingredients, and constantly having sand *everywhere*).

So instead, we like to have people define their ideal every day experience. What's the difference?

Where your ideal day might be sitting on the beach, getting a massage with a pina colada in hand, your ideal everyday experience describes how you want each day to look for you to allow you to achieve your ideal lifestyle.

In order to do this, take a week and think about what your ideal schedule/ routine would be. Consider the following:

- What time do you want to wake up each day?
- What do you want your morning routine to look like?
- How much time do you want to spend working?
- What sort of self-care do you want to practice (ex. eating, exercise, meditation, etc.)?
- What time do you want to set aside for hobbies?

Also, you can think in terms of the five F's (Family, Friends, Fitness, Finance, and Fulfillment).

When you know that your ideal lifestyle and your ideal everyday experience looks like, you can then proceed to determine the gaps and how to get started making it a reality.

Define What You Need to Do

Thinking back to the analogy of your life like a GPS, we have knocked out the first item.

~~Step 1 – Enter your destination~~ Check!

So you can now move on to the next step, which is defining your starting point and plotting out a roadmap/course to guide you towards our vision. For each item or category on your vision board/Ideal Everyday Experience, you want to describe where you currently are in relation to those items. For example:

Let's say that you want to leave your job. (**Destination**)

Today you are currently working a job. You work 45 hours a week and make $50,000/year. (**Starting Point**)

So now all that's left is defining the milestones to go from your *starting point* to your *destination*. Here are some ideas to consider to help you identify the key changes to make to reach your goal:

- What logical steps do you need follow? You can do some research to find out how people typically accomplish this goal.
- What have other people who have achieved this goal successfully done? Find people who have achieved the goal and ask them how they did it and for their advice.

In the case of leaving a job, these might be some of the key changes: (**Changes Required**)

- Determine how to reduce living expenses to $40,000/year (i.e. instead of $4,000 a month we cut down to $3,000 a month) so I don't have to make as much money to leave my job

- Determine how to use the extra money to pay off debt and start building some savings
- Determine how to make the money required to replace my job

This now helps you clarify the destination, the starting point and some key actions/milestones that would be required to make the shift. Let's look at another example:

Let's say that the car you want to have is a 2018 Mercedes Benz E400. You do some research and determine that this car costs $58,000 and has a monthly payment of $1,000. **(Destination)**

Today you currently drive a 2010 Toyota Camry LE. It is valued at $8,000 and you owe $2,000 left on your car loan (net value to you of $6000). **(Starting Point)**

Changes to make: **(Changes Required)**

- Pay off current car loan (immediate cost of $2,000)
- Save $58,000 or generate an additional $1,000/month in income to cover the car payment
- Sell the Toyota Camry and use the profit as a down payment on the Mercedes E400

By doing this exercise, you've now shown yourself all the key elements needed to start the process of reaching your goal; that you currently drive a 2010 Toyota Camry LE with a $2,000 car loan balance but you want to be driving a 2018 Mercedes Benz E400, which costs $58,000. In order to make the change, you need to pay off your current car loan, figure out a way to either save $58,000 or a way to generate an additional $1,000/month for the car payment and finally sell your current car. You will want to continue going through this process with each of the major areas and/or items on your vision board and ideal every day.

Creating Your Roadmap/Timeline

After defining your *destination*, your *starting point* and *changes required* for each aspect, you now want to combine them together into a single roadmap (*plan*). For this, you will take the major categories of your vision board and lay them out (you will use your completed worksheet from Chapter 1.2 for this).

Then you will take the goals within each category (ex. leave your job) and put them on the ideal timeframe for when you want that goal to happen (ex. 3 years).

LIFE PLANNER ROADMAP

3 YEARS	2 YEARS	1 YEAR			
		90 DAYS	90 DAYS	90 DAYS	90 DAYS
START	STOP	CONTINUE	DO MORE	DO LESS	
PERSONAL NET WORTH:					

This is a sketch of the second page of the Life Planner, the Roadmap.
Available at lifestylebuildersbook.com

The timeframes on your roadmap can adjust, but you want to be sure to include short, medium, and long-term timeframes. So you may use 1 year, 3 years, and 5 years. You could also look out longer and include 10 years (or even break it down more over the next 1 to 5 years). Do what works for you. The timeframe is less important than the layout of your goals.

One thing that we do recommend for everyone, regardless of the specific timeframe that you choose, is to break the next year into 90 days increments, each with their own goals. (We will dive into this more in subsequent sections of the book, but this practice will help you break down your goals and focus on achieving smaller goals and reflecting/adjusting every 90 days as you work towards your vision. Breaking it down in these small pieces helps in a couple ways: 1. Giving yourself small achievements towards a bigger goal keeps you motivated and less overwhelmed and 2. Smaller time frames give you some flexibility to adjust if needed as you go along). Continue this process with each goal. This will create a visual map of where you want to be (vision) and the key goals/steps in order that will get you to your vision.

You may find as you start placing goals in time windows that some windows might be overloaded, and you may need to shift some goals around (forward or backward on your roadmap). It is common for us to want everything now, but often that is not realistic (unless you have unlimited resources, which most of us don't). It's much better to focus on a few goals, and once complete, then moving on to the next logical goals.

As you create/review this roadmap with your spouse/family, you will likely find that you have different thoughts on not only the goals, but also the timeframes. This is where it will be beneficial to refer back to your purpose/vision and use that to guide the discussions. Also, a useful activity that we used was to engage in open conversation about what was important to us individually and as a family and allow fluidity in moving goals around until we were happy with the course forward. Asking some of the following conversations can help work through disagreements over goals or timeframes.

- Which items does each person hold as non-negotiable? We call these items "off the table". By having each person consider what their top priorities/must haves are, it then makes it easier to discuss/adjust the less important goals that are left "on the table" for negotiations. For example, in one of our early discussions, we discussed downgrading our living conditions to free up money in our budget. Tom was considering selling our house and renting for a time, but owning our own home was a non-negotiable item for Ariana, so we nixed the renting idea and moved on to other ways to free up money in our budget.

- Can this item move forward or backward in the timeline? Sometimes the item is important for you to achieve, but the timing may be off. In this case, see if you can shift when you want to achieve this item. For example, if one person wants to leave their job. Doing this will reduce your overall income, so rather than getting rid of this goal, you may be able to move it back in the timeline to allow more time to build your business and replace your income. So discuss and decide on the right timeframe for this goal.

- Can you break this goal up into pieces or steps? Sticking with the leaving the job example from above, consider alternatives. One option might be to switch to a different job in the short term that you enjoy more. Another option is to reduce your hours at your job or switch to a part-time job. This would still allow some income to come in, while also freeing up time to build the business. So, define and evaluate alternative approaches and how you can break the goal up.

Once you have made any shifts and are happy with the timing, then you want to start looking at the changes required for each goal and map those into timeframes to achieve your goal. For example:

Goal: to leave your job

Plan: In the next 90 days you will reduce your living expenses so that you can live on $40,000/year instead of $50,000. This means that you need to bring home $3,333/month to cover your expenses.

You don't want to break this down any further at this point, but now you know the key focus for the next 90 days to move towards this goal.

> *Important Side Note: There is a lot more to consider financially when leaving your job. Some of your expenses may go down (ex. spending less on gas), but some will also go up (ex. you will have to pay for your own health insurance, and you will pay more in taxes because of self-employment tax. We dive much deeper into this scenario and what you need to do in the "Find Your Freedom" section of the book. This section walks through the process to help you crunch the numbers in an easy way to know exactly how much you need to bring home, how much you need to have saved, how much your business needs to make and how to plan it all out. Many people leave their jobs too soon and end up sabotaging their business, so be sure to spend some time with the activities in this section so that you don't become one of them.*

First 90 Days Plan: Educate yourself on different businesses that you could start to begin replacing your income.

Second 90 Days Plan: Take one business idea and begin testing it. (The "Concept to Cash" section of this books will walk you through this entire process.)

Third 90 Days Plan: Sell your initial $5,000 with your business.

One Year Mark Plan: Business consistently generating $1,000/month.

Two Year Plan: Business to be consistently generating $2,000/month.

Three Year Plan: Business to be consistently generating $4,000/month with $20,000 in savings so that you can leave your job.

Repeat this process for each goal and you will end up with a consolidated roadmap (plan) for where you want to go, where you are today and the key changes/milestones that you need to accomplish along the way to make it happen. For each of the timeframes, it can also be useful to define your "Monthly Lifestyle Cost." That is, what do you anticipate your monthly expenses being in order to live that lifestyle at that period of time. This helps you shift goals around as needed and determine how you will make that much money to achieve your goals.

With your roadmap now laid out, you have your initial plan for how you will close the gap and begin moving towards your ideal lifestyle. But before you move on, I want you to ask yourself two questions: What is preventing you from living your ideal lifestyle today? What things could you begin doing right now?

Making Changes Today

Often times we think we need to wait and achieve something, but more often than not you can instantly make changes to your routine/lifestyle to begin living closer to your Ideal Everyday Experience. This is similar to the survive versus thrive mode. You don't have to be in just one or the other. Just like you can bring elements of thrive into survive mode, you can begin bringing elements of your Ideal Everyday Experience into your days today. For example, if your Ideal Everyday Experience has you waking up early, see how you can begin doing that now. Think along the terms of the 1%. How can you begin waking up 15 minutes earlier starting tomorrow? Set your alarm clock? Have a task that needs to be completed early? Sometimes routine can help. Consistent small actions can lead to amazing results when done consistently over time.

Or if you want to begin eating healthier to lose weight, think about what you can begin implementing right now. According to WedMD[2], a simple trick is to drink more water before you eat a meal.

Want to spend more time with your family? Plan out your week and put the most important activities on there first. Every week when we plan our calendar, the first items to get booked in are our personal and family time.

Want to save more money? Track and review where you spent your money last month and identify expenses to cut or swap out. You can cancel subscriptions that you are no longer using, reduce eating out and cook more at home.

You are probably a lot closer to being able to do some of these things than you realize. Instead of saying that you can't have them now, start asking yourself *how* you can have small pieces them now. Making that small shift can have a huge impact on your ability to see how you can have more now.

Create Your Process: Reflect and Adjust

The first two steps were fun, although they were probably more challenging than you initially thought and took longer than you anticipated. This is normal. You've got to envision the future and think about all of the cool stuff that you will build into your life *before* you set out to accomplish it. You have a cool vision board and roadmap defined for how you will make it all a reality. You have even taken small steps (and are waking up 15 minutes earlier than you were before). But now is the time to implement your roadmap and work toward your Ideal Everyday Experience.

And this is also where people who never leave that 45-hour-a-week-job stop.

Have you ever watched people set New Year's resolutions? Or maybe you have set some yourself? You get all excited, make a plan, and hit the ground running on January 1st. All is good for a few days, then a bump in the road happens (pun completely intended). You get sick. A family member needs your help unexpectedly. There's a rerun of "Friends" on that you haven't seen in a while and figure you can catch up on your goal tomorrow. And suddenly things get off track and two weeks later you have stopped working towards your goal.

We don't want this to happen to you. Step 3 is where we begin really differentiating this Plan With Purpose process from traditional goal-setting (because traditional goal-setting rarely works). You see, you need to define and implement a process that works for you and will let you implement (and, more importantly, adjust) your goals as you go. Just like a GPS, you need to check in and recalculate your route based on what happens.

Set Your Check-in Points

Have you ever noticed mile markers when you are driving down a major highway? These are used to identify your location and confirm you are on the right path. If the markers indicate that you are not on the right path, you adjust. You want to do the same thing with your roadmap with check-in points. By setting check-in points, you will have the opportunity to reflect and evaluate your progress while also making adjustments and planning out what to do next.

Here is a starting point that you should consider incorporating into your own process.

Annual Check-In

Most people do an annual check-in, often as the end of the year approaches. They reflect on the year and set some resolutions for the upcoming year. Unfortunately, folks often stop here, not taking action on their proposed goals.

Doing an annual (once-a-year) check-in is a great practice. Not only does it allow you to reflect on the prior year and plan the upcoming year, but also it is an opportunity to step back and look at the big picture. This is a time for you to review your vision and your progress towards it. You may find that some things on your roadmap need to move up or move back. You may have some new goals to add or some that need to be removed or adjusted because they are no longer valid.

Most people prefer to do their annual check-in somewhere near the end of the year, but it doesn't have to be. As long as it is consistent, you can choose anytime of the year to do this. Another great option is June, when people are often less busy with holidays and other year-end activities.

Topics to Consider:
- **Reflect on the previous year.** Create a list of wins (what went well), challenges (what didn't go well) and come out with a small list of adjustments to make in the upcoming year to create more wins and minimize/overcome the losses.
- **Update your roadmap.** Take a look at the various goals that you have listed and make any changes/adjustments recommended from your reflection. Move goals forward or backward, add/remove goals and break down goals as needed.

- **Plan out the upcoming year.** Define a small list of goals for the year (3-5 for your personal life and 3-5 for your business). Break the current year into 4 buckets (90 days each) and break down your big goals into smaller goals/milestones that fit into each bucket. A great question to ask yourself is, *What do I want things to look like one year from now on December 31st when I reflect back?*

Desired Outcome: Clarity and an updated plan. You should have made any updates to your vision and roadmap and specifically have key goals laid out for the year with milestones broken down by 90-day chunks.

By going through this activity each year, you will not only provide yourself with the time to reflect, learn and let go of the previous year, but you will also be able to make adjustments and get clear and focused on what is most important in the upcoming year.

90-Day Check-in (Quarter)

After going through your annual planning, you will now have some goals and milestones for each 90 days (you may also hear them referred to as "quarters", or Q1 Q2 Q3 & Q4 in the business world).

This makes it much easier to do your 90-day check-in. Whereas your annual check-in was focused on the prior year, the longer-term future and the upcoming year, the quarterly check-in is just focused on reflecting on the previous 90 days and adjusting your plan for the next 90 days.

When: Once a quarter. This is generally done near the end of each quarter of the year (December 31, March 30, June 30, September 30).

Topics to Consider:

- **Reflect on the previous quarter.** Create a list of wins (what went well), challenges (what didn't go well) and come out with a small list of adjustments to make in the upcoming quarter to make sure you are on track to meet your annual goals.
- **Plan out the upcoming quarter.** Review and adjust the goals you initially planned out for the upcoming quarter. Again, this should be a small list of 3-5 for your personal life and 3-5 for your business. Then go a step deeper and define the key 3-5 actions that you need to do to achieve each goal and establish a high-level schedule for the quarter.

Desired Outcome: Clarity and an updated plan. You will now have an understanding of your goals, the key activities to focus on to achieve them, and an initial schedule for the next 90 days. This will help you focus and avoid getting distracted.

By going through this activity each quarter, you allow yourself time to reflect and adjust. This is the key to actually achieving your annual goals.

Monthly

With your quarterly planning complete, you now have clarity on your focus and key activities for the next 90 days.

A quarter consists of 3 months. Therefore, doing a check-in each month will allow you to make adjustments along the way to achieve your 90-day goals. It will also allow you to review your key metrics and plan out your monthly budget.

When: Once a month. This is generally done at the end of the month so that you have current data on your KPIs (key performance indicators) as well as your financial information.

Topics to Consider:

- **Review your Progress.** Review if you are on track or off track to achieve your 90-day goals. Review your key metrics for each goal and determine if you need to make any adjustments in order to achieve your 90-day goals.
- **Establish your monthly cash-flow plan.** Each month you should create a cash-flow plan, which defines how much money you anticipate coming in and how you plan to spend it. Some people may also call this a budget. A budget is not restricting. In fact, it is freeing and allows you to be *intentional* with your money and make better decisions.

Desired Outcome: Clarity and an updated plan. You will now have an understanding of how you are progressing on your goals and any adjustments that you need to make to achieve them. You will also have clarity on your money and a roadmap for how much money you plan to bring in over the next month and how to allocate it to your different priorities.

By going through this monthly activity, you can make the smaller adjustments required to achieve your 90-day goals. It also provides you the opportunity to review your finances and plan out your budget for the upcoming month. This is a missing piece for most people and causes them to get into debt and make poor decisions because they don't have an accurate picture of their finances (both personal and business).

Weekly

Your weekly meeting is the heartbeat of your life and business. When you plan out your week, you can get down to the specific tasks that you need to complete. This is a great opportunity to utilize your calendar.

You can plan out specific time or blocks of time so that you know day-by-day and hour-by-hour what you should be focused on. For example:

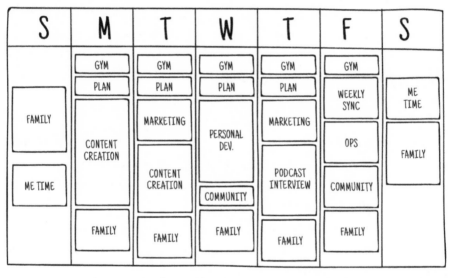

An example of a weekly calendar with planning blocks.

Just like with a budget, some people feel like this is restrictive, but it is actually very freeing! It allows you to be intentional with your time and spend it in the best way to create the lifestyle that you want and to achieve your goals.

When: Once a week. The day doesn't matter, as long as it works for you and is consistent. (We prefer Friday Mornings Wednesdays.)

Topics to Consider:

- **Report and check in on metrics.** Review your key metrics and any key activities that happened during the week. Also, spend some time defining what things went well and what could be improved. Then define a few actions to focus on this week to improve upon issues from the prior week.

- **Plan out your upcoming week.** With an understanding of the prior week and where you stand with your metrics, you can now plan out and break down the top priority items that you need to focus on/complete this week.

Desired Outcome: Clarity and an updated plan. You will now have your upcoming week planned out. This makes it so much easier to be productive and knock out the right activities because you have planned them in advance.

Traditionally people get very detailed in their 90-day plans, mapping out every task for every week. But then as things changed, they would spend a lot of time planning and re-planning. By having higher level plans and implementing this weekly meeting to break them down into tasks, you can reduce the time you spend on planning and allow you to adjust to whatever comes up.

Daily

Last, but not least, is the daily check-in. This meeting allows you to connect and clarify your intentions for the day. By doing this, you can make sure that you are clear on what you need to do and not waste time or get distracted by things that you shouldn't be focused on.

When: Once a day. It doesn't matter what time, so long as it's consistent (just like everything else). We meet in the morning and call our daily meeting "drink up and sync up"—we drink our caffeine and plan out our day.

Topics to Consider:

- **Items completed yesterday.** Review key items that were completed the prior day. This is also a great way to keep others updated (spouses or team members in your business) and also to keep all of you accountable.

- **Focus for today.** Set your key intentions for the day. This allows you to get a clear picture and understand what other people plan to work on.

- **Collaboration for barriers.** Define if there is anyone that you need to work with or if there is anything getting in your way. That way, you can coordinate those discussions or get help with something blocking your progress.

Desired Outcome: Clarity and an updated plan. You now have clarity on your day as well as those around you. You also can make sure that you have the coordination or help to make your day productive.

These daily meetings should be short (15 minutes or fewer). They are not meant to be a full information dump, but instead, are meant to allow you to focus and collaborate quickly so you can be off to the rest of your day (accomplishing your daily goals).

When we first describe this process to people, they usually tell us one of two things: 1) This would take too much time (that they don't have); and 2) This is too structured for their creative spirit.

What they come to learn is that these meetings will actually *save* you time. Many people don't realize how much time they waste doing the wrong tasks, getting sidetracked with non-important actions, waiting to speak to someone or to have a roadblock removed so they can continue. These meetings help avoid and adjust to each of those, actually saving you that time. When done correctly, they will take roughly 10% of your time, but save you many times more what they take.

In terms of creativity, following this structure will actually allow you to be *more* creative. You can define and get clear on what needs to be done, as well as intentionally set aside time to be creative. This creative time then doesn't get sucked into some of the other distractions and time wasters mentioned above.

Remember, this is a starting point, and we recognize that all people operate differently and there are other paths to achieve desired results. But this is the path that worked for us and helped us reach our Ideal Everyday Experience.

Prioritize & Implement

Everything up to this point has helped you lay the foundation and get the structure in place. This does take some time to do, but as with most things, a little bit of planning and foundational work up front then makes it so much easier to execute and get stuff done. Don't skip it.

Seriously, don't skip it!

Before we go too much further, let's first break down what we mean when we discuss being effective vs. being efficient.

To be *effective* means to accomplish a goal or outcome; doing the *right* thing.

To be *efficient* means to perform in a manner with the least amount of waste; doing things with the least amount of time, money, and effort.

When it comes to productivity, many people first focus on becoming more efficient. This is the wrong way to look at things, as the following quote indicates.

> *"There is nothing so useless as doing efficiently that which should not be done at all."*
> Peter Drucker

If you do not first focus on doing the right activities (being effective), it almost doesn't matter how fast you do them (being efficient), as you will just achieve the wrong result faster. You first want to figure out what the right thing to be doing is, and often you *want* to do it inefficiently in the beginning—and here's why.

"Seriously Tom, you want me to do this manually?
But it would be so much faster if I just bought this tool to automate it."

The key thing is that it often takes time to figure out what is effective, so we don't want to focus on creating efficiency until we find out what is effective. This means that you will want to choose the simplest tools and to do something early on (i.e. using pen & paper instead of your computer). This often means manually doing things rather than using tools/technology. Once you are doing the right thing and getting the desired outcome, then you can focus on making things more efficient. As we often say, early on, *do the things that won't scale.* You won't do them this way forever, but it is the best way to get started. Doing things manually is the easiest way to get started and allows you to really understand what needs to be done before you try to make it more efficient.

Thus far we've covered the first step major steps towards being effective, which is helping you clarify what's important in your life and what goals you want to achieve. This will help you make sure that you are focused on the right activities and headed in the right direction. With that complete, we can now actually get in and use this foundation to begin implementing everything that you need to start making progress on your goals and moving towards your vision.

We will take you through a simple process as we do this:

1. Perform a Brain Dump
2. Categorize Your Thoughts
3. Prioritize Your Tasks
4. Plan Your Week
5. Execute!

Perform a Brain Dump

As you begin this process you may find yourself overwhelmed. You have such a backlog of things that you need to do for your life, your job, and your business if you already have one. Given that, it can be difficult to know where to begin.

If this is the case, a brain dump should be your first step. (This is one of Ariana's favorite things to do when she gets overwhelmed, or anytime we are planning out a new project.)

A brain dump is exactly what it sounds like; a dump of everything in your brain. For example, you take a piece of paper, a whiteboard, or your favorite notes app and start dumping all the thoughts and tasks that are on your mind that you need to get done (remember how we said to keep things simple?) This helps achieve a concept known as "mind like water," which refers to a mental and emotional state in which your head is clear, able to create and respond freely, unencumbered with distractions and split focus.

Think of your brain like your browser window, let's say Google Chrome. When you have one or two tabs open on the browser, it functions normally, and you are able to get done what you need to.

But most of us—let's be honest here—have more like 10 or 20 or 30-plus tabs open on Chrome at a time, and then we are surprised when our computer's functionality and speed drop down to a minimum. We are asking Chrome to perform above and beyond its capabilities! That's what we're doing to our brains when we try to keep all those unorganized and chaotic thoughts in our heads. And good luck trying to find the tab that you need.

So now with an understanding of "mind like water," how do you go about achieving it? Schedule some time to put towards this—an hour should do. Take the first 15 minutes and just let things flow. Write down everything that you believe you have to do and anything else that is on your mind. The goal of this step is to get it all out of your head. Getting this out of your head will allow you to free up much needed mental space and allow you to move onto the next step.

When doing this brain dump, be sure to keep your goals handy and make sure that you've included the key actions required to allow you to achieve those goals in the list of things to do. At the end of your brain dump, you will have a list of tasks, thoughts, and ideas that were previously in your head.

Categorize Your Thoughts

After performing your brain dump, the next step is to categorize everything that you listed. One of the reasons we like using Post-It notes for this activity is because we can easily add, remove, and arrange them. At the highest level, you can group your activities by personal, your job, and your business (if you have all three). You can the break them down further into sub-categories if that helps.

Breaking things up this way will allow you to see where your time is potentially being spent and where you believe you need to focus. For example, if you have a lot of thoughts/tasks for your job or business, it may be a sign that you need to focus and either delete, delegate, or automate some of those tasks.

Prioritize Your Tasks

With the list of items now grouped, the next step is to prioritize them. For this, we use something called the Eisenhower Box or Eisenhower Matrix. This process was used by Dwight D. Eisenhower, the 34th President of the United States.

"What is important is seldom urgent
and what is urgent is seldom important."
Dwight Eisenhower

The quadrant was the secret behind Dwight's productivity and has been one of the foundational productive practices of many successful people. Here is how you use it:

For each task that you have to do, figure out which quadrant in the matrix that it falls into.

1. **Urgent & Important (Do First):** These things should be done right away. When planning out your day, these items should be at the top of your list. When this is combined with productivity techniques such as using pomodoros (short periods of intense work followed by a small break) or kanban (focusing on a single task at a time), it can be incredibly powerful. Some example of things that fall into this category could be crises, emergencies, deadlines, impactful issues (i.e. paying your mortgage, sending a client a new contract).

2. **Important & Less Urgent (Schedule):** These tasks are important but may not need to be done right away. These tasks you should schedule and include as part of your weekly planning meeting. Some example of things that fall into this category could be planning, preventing emergencies/issues, personal growth, family time. (i.e. working out, keeping your business books updated)

3. **Urgent & Less Important (Delegate):** These tasks are urgent but are not important. These tasks should be looked at as prime candidates for automation and/or delegation. Some example of things that fall into this category could be interruptions, distractions, and other requests for your attention. (i.e. answering an unknown phone call, checking business email)

4. **Less Urgent & Less Important (Don't Do):** These tasks are less urgent and less important. This is often hard for most people to consider, but these tasks should be either minimized or ignored. Some example of things that fall into this category could be time wasters, procrastination, aimless social media/web browsing. (i.e. constantly checking your phone, in life or business)

Below is a sketch of the box.

THE EISENHOWER BOX

	URGENT	NOT URGENT
IMPORTANT	DO	DECIDE
NOT IMPORTANT	DELEGATE	DELETE

Adapted from Eisenhower, 2012,
Retrieved from https://www.eisenhower.me/eisenhower-matrix/.
Copyright 2011-2017 by EISENHOWER.

By looking at each item in your brain dump/task list and going through this prioritization process, you can quickly label each task with a priority and determine what action you should be taking.

Plan Your Week

Once you have everything prioritized, the next step is to then plan your tasks for the week and begin working on them. To do this, you will use a simple Kanban (also known as scrum) board.

Scrum is a set of principles and practices to help be more productive and more adaptive to changes. It comes from Rugby and is used to help people and businesses plan and focus their work. A big part of its effectiveness is because it is a visual board (either a physical board or an electronic one) that allows you to move your tasks through various states as you work on them.

Here is how you set it up and use it:

Step 1 – Create a board with 3 columns – To-Do, Doing, Done. This can be created using a wall, some painters tape, and Post-It notes, which we recommend for everyone that we work with that are just getting started. It can also be done with an electronic tool that has a Scrum board. There are many tools out there, but don't get caught up in finding the perfect tool. A wall or the electronic tool is all you need.

Step 2 – Populate the To-Do column with your prioritized list of tasks.

Step 3 – When you begin your work, move the top card (task) from the To-Do column and into the Doing column.

Step 4 – Continue working on this task until you complete it. At that point, move it from the Doing column to the Done column.

Step 5 – Continue this process with the next task.

SIMPLE SCRUM BOARD

TO-DO	DOING	DONE

Here is an example of a basic Scrum board.

Note: There is more to Scrum than what I've described here, but this will get you started. So create your board, prioritize your tasks (focused on one week's work at a time) and limit your work-in-progress to no more than three tasks at one time.

At this point, you should be ready to dive in and get to work. You've dumped everything out of your head, used your goals to help you prioritize all of those tasks and have now established a simple process to see your prioritized list of work that allows you to focus on only a few of those items as a time.

There is one additional strategy that we love to use as we plan out our week: organizing and blocking off time in our calendars. This is actually the first thing we do when we plan out our week. You can use either an electronic calendar or a physical calendar for this.

When using a calendar, one challenge that many people have is it can get crowded and it's not easy to see what all of your different events are for. To solve this, create a few categories for the types of things that you will put on your calendar, such as personal time, family time, and business time. This can be done on most electronic tools with categories and can be done physically by color coding your calendar.

Below are the calendars that we currently use.

- One calendar for each member of our family, as well as one for combined family activities.
- One calendar for each business that we own.

You can use as many or as few calendars as you want. The key is being able to organize different types of activities. At a minimum, we'd recommend at least two calendars; one for personal items and one for business items.

With that, as part of your weekly planning session, you can then plan out your calendar and any key activities. You first want to place any personal items on your calendar. This makes sure that you are keeping your personal and family items as a top priority and planning them first.

With your important items now planned out, you can then begin planning time for business activities. This is what we call *work/life integration* (as opposed to work/life balance). You plan your life, then integrate work in between it to support your Ideal Everyday Experience. It's possible that you may not currently have as much flexibility in these areas as you want, and you may have to do certain job or business functions at certain times. But one of the reasons that you are reading this book is to help you set things up so that you have more control and flexibility in this area.

Track Your Progress

You are now ready to dive in and get to work. You've got your basic processes and tools established so that you know what you will focus on (and when). But with all of this planning—and with all the work that you will be doing—how do you know that it is actually moving you *towards* your goal? Without defining some key metrics, this can be a challenge. Now some people get scared when we mention metrics, but we are going to show you a simple process for both identifying the right metrics to track and some simple ways to track them. Remember when we discussed the mile markers on the highway (mile markers identify where you are on your path and help you see when you need to adjust)? These metrics that you use will be your mile markers.

What Metrics Do You Track?

There are so many potential options to track that it is often difficult to pick the right metrics and not get overwhelmed. To get our first metric, you will want to think about the end result that you want to achieve. For example, if your goal is to lose weight, how much weight to do you ultimately want to lose? If you want to make more money in your business, how much money do you want to make?

As you can see, if you know that you want to achieve a certain result, it becomes easy to identify your first metric. For losing weight, you may want to lose 15 pounds. For making more money, it might be making an extra $5,000/month.

To make this even easier, I recommend using the following format when setting your goals:

"I want to go from X to Y by Z."

Ex. "I want to go from weighing 200 pounds to 185 pounds by July 1st."

By framing your goals this way, you can easily tell your starting point, your destination and the timeframe. You first metric then becomes your destination. This is known as a *lagging* metric. This type of metric will let you know if you have achieved the result, but only after the fact. For example, if you step on the scale and realize that you've only lost 3 pounds when you ideally should've lost 5 pounds, you will know where you stand (that mile marker) but you can't do anything to change the result now.

So in addition to defining a lagging metric, you also want to define at least one *leading* metric. A leading metric will track the activity that will lead to the lagging metric. A key characteristic of a leading metric is that you can influence it to help achieve the lagging metric. For example, in order to lose 15 pounds, what key actions do you need to do? Well, you lose weight when you take in fewer calories than your body needs daily, or when you expend more calories than your body needs. To take in fewer calories, you could track how many calories you eat each day. You may target to take in 1,900 calories a day when your body needs 2,200 a day, meaning that you have a 300 calorie deficit. To simplify this process, you could prepare three 500-calorie meals and four 100-calorie snacks for the day. Then you simply track when you eat them. Or if you don't want to track calories, you could restrict your eating time by following something like Intermittent Fasting, where you fast most of the day and only consume calories during a specific window. These two options will help limit the amount of calories that you take in.

To expend more calories, you could track how many calories you expend each day through various activities like walking and exercise. Given that this is a little more complicated, you could track how many times you work out or how many steps you take, knowing that each workout or increase in steps will expend calories (there are tons of apps out there that help with this, as well as products like the "FitBit"). You can then get a rough idea of how many calories are expended with each activity and use that as a guide.

By tracking these two metrics, you should be able to predict if the scale will show an increase or decrease in our weight.

For a business example, you may want to make $2,500 a week. How do you do this? Well, if you sell a $500 product or service, you have to sell 5 of these products ($2,500/$500). So how do you sell these products? Well, you might reach out to people who are interested in a similar product and have a phone call with them.

Weekly Goal	Product/Service Price	# to Sell/Week
$2,500	$500	5

Let's assume that for every 4 people that you talk to, one of them purchases your product. So to sell one product ($500), you need to talk to 4 people. Therefore in order to sell $2,500, you need to talk to 20 people (assuming that 1/4 or 25% of the people that you talk to purchase).

Conversion Rate to Customer	# of People to Talk To
25% (1 out of 4)	20

In order to talk to 20 people on the phone, you need to reach out and request a phone call. If 1 out of every 5 people you reach out to agrees to get on the phone, that means you will have to reach out to ~100 people to get 20 people on the phone.

Conversion Rate to Phone Call	# of People Offer a Call To
20% (1 out of 5)	100

So your leading metric to track should be # of people that you reach out to. Assuming you know your conversion rate, you should be able to predict how many sales you will make based on the # of people who you reach out to. For example, in the above scenario, if you offer 100 people a phone call, that will mean you should make 5 sales for a total of $2,500. If you offered 200 people a phone call, that should lead to 10 sales for a total of $5,000.

You should be tracking these metrics each day (ex. during your daily check-in) as well as during your weekly check-in. If you get to your weekly check-in and you weren't able to hit your goal, you can then reflect and make adjustments so that you can have more success the next week.

This is just a brief introduction to these concepts of leading and lagging metrics. For a further deep dive into them and a great system for how to achieve your goals, check out the book *The 4 Disciplines of Execution: Achieving Your Wildly Important Goals by Chris McChesney and Sean Covey*. The book is focused on achieving business goals, but we have incorporated many of the concepts into achieving personal goals as well.

Qualitative vs. Quantitative Metrics

The other thing to consider as you define and track metrics is understanding and using both qualitative and quantitative metrics.

Quantitative metrics are those metrics that you can count. The metrics that we defined above, such as tracking your weight loss and calories burned are examples of quantitative metrics. They provide hard statistics but little insight behind them. An easy way to think about these metrics is that you can put them in a spreadsheet and generate a graph from them.

Qualitative metrics, on the other hand, provide less hard data but allow for a deeper level of insights and understanding. This data is often messy and hard to aggregate but provides answers to the question "why." These are typically free-form responses from people, which you can't easily track in a spreadsheet, but give you a lot more information to explain the data that you can track in a spreadsheet. For losing weight, this might be jotting down how you feel as you eat your meals and exercise, which can help understand why you reached your weight-loss goal or didn't reach your weight-loss goal. For business, you might keep notes of specific objections that people had as you had sales calls with them so you can better understand your customer and why they did/didn't buy.

So, you want to make sure that you are using the right mix of qualitative metrics to understand "why" things are the way they are, and quantitative metrics so that you can measure "how" and "how much." Anytime you get stuck, focus on some qualitative metrics to help you understand *why* you are stuck and what you need to get unstuck. For example, your mental state can have a lot of influence on your eating habits. If you have a hard week at work, or something happens in your personal life, these could each cause you to fall off on your eating habits, which will in turn affect your overall weight loss for the week. Those emotional factors are qualitative, they can't necessarily be measured but have as much of an affect as the quantitative metrics.

It can take a little bit of time to nail your metrics, and they will likely change with each goal that you have, but once you do, you will make your life (and business) a lot easier to navigate. The metrics will act as a scoreboard and help show you where you are and guide your next move towards your goals.

Distill Who You Need to Be

The last and final step in laying your foundation for success is distilling who you need to be—in other words, how do you need to change and grow as a person to be able to reach your Ideal Everyday Experience? Kudos for making it this far. Seriously. Most people skip over this foundational stuff, and ultimately make everything more difficult as a result. If you are reading this, then you have a drive and commitment to seek out the knowledge that you need to build the life that you desire.

As great as it is that you have gone through the above steps, we have to be real with you: You can go through all of the steps above, but still not achieve the success and lifestyle that you want. Why? Because of *you*. You are the biggest contributor and factor in your success. That also means that *you* are the biggest contributor and factor to your lack of success. It all comes down to who you *are*, how you *think*, and how you *act*.

One of the biggest things that people overlook as they work to achieve their goals is the importance their perspective and mindset has when it comes to achieving success. This journey—and it is a journey—will require you to grow as a person and challenge a lot of what you think you know. It will require you to look inwards at who you are and what stories (also known as "limiting beliefs") you are telling yourself. Each level of success requires more growth, and this growth begins now as you have your roadmap laid out and you are figuring out who you need to *be* in order to *do* the things that you need to do to *have* the success, life, and business that you desire.

And this step will help you gain clarity around what that looks like now and what it needs to look like in order for you to achieve success.

Victim vs. Victor Paradigm

Our paradigms are how we view the world. Think of them as a set of glasses that you are wearing. Depending on the glasses, the world may look different, even though it is the same. For example, while wearing dark shaded sunglasses it will make the world look dark but change it out for a set of red tinted glasses and will give everything a rosy look. The world is the same in both scenarios, but how you see it varies a lot depending on your perspective and paradigm.

Everyone has their own paradigm, but at the highest level, successful people can often be grouped into one overarching paradigm and unsuccessful people into another. People who are not successful often have a *Victim Paradigm*. In this case, they often see themselves as a victim and lay blame on their situation or others as the reasons that they are not successful. For example, they might say that someone else is successful because their family had money, or because they went to an Ivy League school. They look for excuses. They are always "too busy" (often with non-important activities) or their circumstances won't allow them to be successful. They say they *can't* be successful. They take away all of their own power and give the power to their current circumstances and therefore often are not able to create their own success.

Now, successful people often have a different paradigm, a *Victor Paradigm*. They realize that they are in control of their lives and the outcomes. They may not be able to control everything that happens, but they can control their *response* and *reaction* to what happens. They make sacrifices (instead of excuses) to get to where they want to be and find time for what is important. They are willing to admit that they made a mistake and take action to overcome obstacles that get in their way.

Going through the previous chapters will make little-to-no difference in your life if you have a Victim Paradigm as you will always find an excuse for why you can't achieve your goals and why things won't/didn't work out for you. In order to truly benefit from them, you need to have the Victor Paradigm and be willing to take control of your life and what happens in it.

Be – Do – Have

Speaking of paradigms, there is an additional way that successful people look at things (which is often the opposite of unsuccessful people). Zig Ziglar, the author, salesman, and motivational speaker, preached his philosophy around the concept of Be – Do – Have. Simply put, you have to *Be* the right kind of person to *Do* the right things so that you can *Have* what you desire in life.

Unsuccessful people look at things from the Have-Do-Be perspective. They may say…

"I need to have more money, then I could start a business to do the necessary things to leave my job, which would allow me to be happy."

This falls back into that victim paradigm Unsuccessful people are making an excuse (if they only had more money), then they would be able to do something, at which point they would be happy. But of course they will never have enough money, therefore they cannot do the things to leave their job, and thus they will not be able to be happy.

But successful people look at things differently. They may say:

"I want to have the ability to leave my job, so what I must do is create a business that allows for that. In order to create a successful business, I need to be a person who can find and sell a solution to people that experience a certain problem."

See the difference? In the first example, the person was not thinking about who they needed to be/how they needed to think to have success. No, instead they were focused on what they didn't have, which then prevented them from being able to do the required actions. That prevented them from being successful and happy.

In the second example, the person focused on who they needed to be in order to do the things they needed to do in order to have the success that they wanted to have (Be – Do – Have). They defined what they wanted to have (like you did in Chapter 1.2 - Describe What You Want to Have and Chapter 1.3 - Define What You Need to Do), figured out what they needed to do (like you did in Chapter 1.4 - Create Your Process, Chapter 1.5 - Prioritize & Implement, and Chapter 1.6 - Track Your Progress) and figured out who they needed to be (like you are doing in this chapter).

Think about this: You defined what you wanted to have above (your life vision and your ideal every day). You defined what you needed to do (your goals, milestones and key actions). Now you need to figure out who you need to be in order to do the things that you described above.

- Do you need to be someone who constantly learns and challenges yourself?
- Do you need to be someone who sees problems as opportunities?
- Do you need to be someone who is able to be vulnerable and ask for help?
- Do you need to be someone who can continue past failure and learn from your mistakes?
- Do you need to be someone who can work with others?

Are the above items accurate for you? What else do you need to be? Once you figure out who you need to be, it will then make it much easier for you to do the things that you need to do in order to have your ideal life.

SWOT Analysis

Another tool that will help you with determining who you need to be is a tool that is traditionally used to analyze businesses, but today we will use it to help you analyze yourself. It's called SWOT analysis.

A SWOT analysis is composed of 4 aspects:

- Internal
  - Strengths (Helpful)
  - Weaknesses (Harmful)
- External
  - Opportunities (Helpful)
  - Threats (Harmful)

By going through and asking yourself what strengths, weaknesses, opportunities, and threats you have, you can better understand yourself and play to your strengths/opportunities and work to mitigate your weaknesses/threats. In addition to doing this yourself, it can also be useful to ask some people close to you their thoughts (check out the resources for an idea of some questions to ask!). Often times we can have blind spots and it can be hard to see some of these things for ourselves, but it can be much easier for others to identify.

Personality Tests

Personality tests are another great tool to use to better understand yourself and may actually help you fill out part of your SWOT analysis. With these tests, you will answer a list of questions, which will typically then generate a rating for you in various categories. This, along with a report, is pretty accurate for how you think/behave and can really help you better understand yourself and how you act. It can also help you understand some of your weaknesses and how to best interact with others.

Here are a few personality tests that you can take to better understand yourself and how you may naturally act. There are many more out there, but these are some of the most effective in helping us not only know ourselves, but also to know each other and other people whom we interact with:

- Myers-Briggs Type Indicator
- DiSC
- Kolbe A
- StrengthFinders
- The Five Love Languages

Taking these tests will help you better understand yourself (some of them are free and others require a small fee. You can find links to each of them in our resources section!). As an added benefit, have your spouse/partner take them as well and exchange results. Ariana and I did, and it really helped us understand more about each other, our natural tendencies and why we act the way we do (which we found wasn't just to frustrate each other). Through this process, we figured out that we were often times complete opposites, which would initially frustrate us and lead to disagreements. Once we took these tests, we not only better understood each other, but we also had an easier time defining which roles we should each embrace in both our lives and our businesses.

Identify Shifts to Make

Once you understand who you are today and who you need to be, you can then identify what changes you need to make to become that person. Look at in your outline of what you need to do to achieve to reach your ideal life and your goals then start reflecting. Take a look at people who are doing what you want to do and who have your desired results. Talk to them, get to know them, work for them, hire them. Do whatever it takes to be around them and really focus on understanding what type of person they needed to be to have their results. Then determine what shifts you need to make to be this person.

Think about:

- What mindsets/perspectives you need to have.
- What new skills you may need to pick up.
- What old skills you have that will be valuable moving forward.
- What new habits you may need to develop.
- What old habits you may need to drop.

The last one is critical. If you want to be successful, you probably don't want to go out and party every weekend. So you may have to shift some of your habits/priorities.

A useful activity for both who you need to be and the tasks that you need to do is called "Start, Stop, Continue, Do More, Do Less." In this simple activity, you look at what you want to achieve and decide what you need to start doing, stop doing, continue doing, do more of, and do less of to get there. We also use this as part of the various check-in activities that we defined earlier in this section (Like your Weekly, Monthly & 90 Day Meetings).

So that's it.

We started this section out with getting clear on *what you wanted to have*, then helped you figure out *what you needed to do* and ended with helping you clarify *who you need to be*.

Don't let this abundance of information overwhelm you. Grab the corresponding Lifestyle Builders Starter Pack over at lifestylebuildersbook.com and allocate some time over the next week to really dive in and map this all out—and get it on the agenda for your daily and weekly meetings!

Finally, start being the person that you need to be to make this all happen. You can do it!

Lifestyle Builder Starter Pack Resource

These Worksheets & Guided Activities will help you organize and define these all of these areas for getting clarity on your life. This is included with your starter pack that you get for free with this book. Get your free copy at www.lifestylebuildersbook.com

Section 2:
Find Your Freedom

Section Summary

With clarity around your ideal life and a roadmap, it's now time to determine what needs to happen to make that happen. You will go through and define your *Freedom Number*—the amount of money that you need to bring in to leave your job. This includes gathering and understanding all of your financial information (from how much you make, to how much you spend, to how much debt you have, and how much money your business need to make in order to allow you to leave your job).

The goal of this section is to help you get your personal finances in order, as well as help you model what your business will need to look like to achieve the vision and goals that you laid out in the previous section.

Can We Really Leave Our Jobs?

Tom's Take

"We can make this work babe. You see, this is how much we make from each duplex that we buy. If we take our current monthly expenses and divide it by the amount of cash that we bring home from each, we can determine the number of duplexes that we need to buy to allow us both to leave our jobs."

That was me trying to convince Ariana that this plan to have us both leave our jobs was feasible. Months earlier, I had spent all of that money on the real estate investment training. After attending the first training, I was frustrated. The "advanced" training really didn't give us an actionable plan nor a lot of substance. In addition, the company was calling me and trying to get me to invest more money into their coaching. The additional three "advanced" trainings were in other areas of the country, which would require many more thousands in travel costs.

I passed on the next three training courses. The $7,500 that I had already spent was a sunk cost, and an expensive lesson. You can imagine how this conversation with Ariana went. Not only did she originally not want us to invest in real estate, I spent $7,500 on a real estate investment training without talking to her. Now I had decided that the training wasn't worth the money (she was going to be thrilled with that news) and I would move forward with real estate investing on my own.

It's amazing that we are still married. It's tough being married to an entrepreneur. We think differently, look at risk differently, make a lot of mistakes, and eventually we fit all of the puzzle pieces together and start finding success.

I realized that I had a lot of what I needed and started with my biggest strength: problem solving. I knew that with some focus and a few supporting resources, I could make this work. I abandoned the "advanced trainings," set a goal to purchase our first real estate investment and put together a plan to make it a reality. I purchased a few books to fill in some gaps in knowledge that I had, such as how to analyze a real estate investment to make sure that we made money. I had also found an online community of real estate investors to help answer specific questions.

So, with that, I set out in search of potential properties to purchase. I created a spreadsheet that would help me analyze deals and began running different investments through it. Not long after, I found someone selling a duplex in the local paper from my home town, which was about an hour away from where Ariana and I lived. As I typed their number into the phone to call and inquiry about the property, I had butterflies in my stomach. I was in my early twenties with a lot of debt, little cash, not really knowing what I was doing, and now calling someone to purchase their property, which I had no idea how I was going to make it happen. I was very nervous, but I made the call. After a few conversations back and forth, we agreed on a purchase price.

Now how the heck are we going to pay for this? I called my father to see if he wanted to partner with me. He had a construction background, was local to the area, and had a few apartments of his own. He wasn't interested. He didn't take me seriously (I think he thought this was some sort of get rich quick attempt on my part, instead of a true attempt to get into real estate. Maybe he was even a little bit offended I had jumped into this without asking him for his opinion/expertise). So I called my cousin, the one who purchased the real estate training with me, and asked if he wanted to partner up. I laid out the numbers for him, explained my plan for running the management of the property, and what the long-term goal was. He said yes, as he also wanted to find a way to pay back the money that he has spent on the training.

I then had to find a bank to give us a mortgage. We didn't really have any money and we had just purchased our own house a few months earlier. Bank after bank turned us down. We were too young. We didn't have experience. The amount we were asking for was "too low" for a mortgage (many banks won't lend you less than $50,000 for a mortgage). I was shocked! I didn't realize having ambition, learning the business, and negotiating a good deal would not be enough for a bank to lend us money.

So as a last-ditch effort, we reached out to a local bank in the area where the property was located. Being as they were local, some of the bank executives knew my family as a part of the small-town community, and they liked the fact that we were investing in the local community. I dressed up in a suit, drove down to the bank to meet with one of the vice presidents, and left with a mortgage! (I of course had also done a lot of research and made sure to walk them through my business plan). After we closed on the property and it was ours, my cousin and I had a mini-celebration.

"Here's the first brick to pave our future!"

When I got home that night, I was so excited to show Ariana the numbers.

"We can make this work babe. You see, this is how much we make from each duplex that we buy. If we take our current monthly expenses and divide it by the amount of cash that we bring home from each, we can determine the number of duplexes that we need to buy to allow us both to leave our jobs."

She looked like a deer in headlights. And she started to cry because she still had fears around this whole real estate investment thing. I was frustrated because I couldn't seem get her on board with my idea. I decided that we didn't need more conversation, we just needed each other. So the rest of the night, we laid in bed, Ariana crying, and me frustrated. Even with all of that, we embraced each other and knowing that we would work through all of this together.

A few nights later, I tried a different approach.

While lying in bed and talking, I nonchalantly asked Ariana what she wanted out of life. This started an amazing discussion of both of us sharing our dreams and the vision for what we wanted our lives to be. Ariana shared some of her dreams, such as us moving into a bigger house and being able to have freedom as we started our family. The next day, we decided to expand on this by each of us writing out what we wanted our life to be like/contain in 10 years, 5 years, 3 years, 1 year and 6 months. We shared our goals and created a combined list that encompassed our most important goals.

This was something that I had not done before, but it led to a huge breakthrough. Instead of just telling Ariana what I wanted (to retire by 35), I also began to tell her why I wanted it (to create an amazing life for us and our future kids). In addition, I asked her what she wanted, and we found that we were aligned on most of what we wanted. This was the first time that we actually wrote these things down and saw each other's responses, and it was powerful.

Once we were aligned, I brought up the idea of real estate again. Even though we both had some fear about it, I walked through a simple example of a duplex.

Purchase Price: $30,000

Down Payment: $6,000

Monthly Rents: $1,000

Monthly Expenses: $500 (Estimate)

Monthly Mortgage: $180

Monthly Cash flow (Profit): $320

Again, as soon as I brought up the numbers, I started to see some fear creep in. It was then that I did something that made all of the difference in the world for her. Instead of talking numbers, I tied this back to the goal that we had just discussed.

"Do you realize that if we purchased 4 of these duplexes, we could replace your income?"

The conversation was now not just about numbers and money, but what that money would allow us to achieve from our list of goals, specifically freedom.

Ariana's Take

I hate numbers. Math was my least favorite subject in. Figuring out anything with complex equations or too many variables is just not my jam. So you can guess that I was also not a fan of handling the "money stuff" in our relationship.

Tom and I grew up very differently, and we each had different relationships with money when we met. I was an only child with two moms who both had pretty good salaries. I never wanted for anything; if I needed it, it appeared! This continued as we became parents, with our daughter informing Tom that if he needed something, he should just ask "MeeMee" and "Gram" (my parents).

College was my first real encounter handling my own finances, but even then I didn't have a job during school (no time for that with science labs and soccer practice!) so we maxed out my student loans to cover my costs of living on/off campus. (If I'd known then what I know now, oh boy would things have been different.)

Tom, on the other hand, had moved out of his family home and gotten his own apartment in high school. He bought his own car, paid his own rent, and worked three jobs some summers to keep himself funded. When he got to college things were no different. He'd saved up money from his jobs to pay for what he needed, or he found ways to make money at school with online poker or his Amazon book business. (He hated taking money from anyone by the way. I used to pay for things for him when I had extra, and it drove him nuts.)

But neither one of us was *really* ready for money in the real world, after college. I remember our first apartment together, sitting on the floor and working on our budget. Divvying up the little money we were making to pay for rent, our vehicles, and of course those lovely student loans.

We had graduated from college with a whopping $66,000 in student loan debt. Plus, we had a couple thousand in credit card debt. And things got worse from there, as we prepared to get married and pay for our wedding. Why not add a home mortgage in there, and maybe a new-to-us car, too?!

At one point, we racked up more than $200,000 in debt. We were 22 and making a combined $56,000 per year. As we tried to pay down that debt year after year, it felt like handcuffs restricting our every move in life. How were we ever going to live our dream of being financially free? How could we ever get to the point when Tom could leave his increasingly high paying job? How were we ever going to reach that dream life we had envisioned for us, and for our kids someday?

For a long time I wasn't sure how to answer any of those questions, which led to a lot of frustration in our relationship. Over time though, Tom's passion to create a better life for ourselves, and his slight shift in communicating *why* he wanted that (instead of continuing to talk about what he wanted to do) opened my eyes to new possibilities.

Determine Monthly Cash Flow Needs

*F*reedom means different things to different people. It might be having certain things, such as a certain house, car or other items. Or it might be certain experiences, such as being able to take vacations or travel across the country. Or maybe it is about the people in your life and the relationships that you have with them. Or maybe it is the ability to have an impact. Maybe you want to donate your time to a cause that you care about, or maybe even start your own non-profit to change the world.

At the end of the day, this simple definition tends to apply to most people.

Freedom = Options

And expanded:

Freedom = Doing What You Want, When You Want, With Whom You Want

That is, the more options you have, the more freedom you have. Most people don't have as many options as they want because certain things control or restrict their life. Typically, this comes down to where their time and energy are spent in the pursuit of making more money.

If you read the first section of this book, Plan With Purpose, you should now have a much clearer picture on what you want out of your life and what freedom means to you. Whatever it is that you seek, it all starts with being able to understand what it will take for you to achieve your own freedom. Remember that Be – Do – Have activity?

For most people, the biggest barrier to achieving true freedom comes from the fact that they have to work a job in order to support themselves (and their family). For most people, their job requires a minimum 40 hours a week. This amount of time increases once you add in commute time and extra time that their job may require. So it is no wonder that many people spend 50, 60 or even more hours per week contributing to their job.

Why do they do this?

For most people, it's because they have expenses and bills that need to be paid. These expenses generally fall into one of the following categories:

- **Pay Yourself First** (before your other expenses get paid): Such as your emergency fund, additional savings, retirement (non-401k), investments, and any college funds for your kids.
- **Housing:** Your mortgage (or rent), your real estate taxes, your home-owner's insurance, maintenance, furnishing, and anything else related to where you live.
- **Utilities:** Your electricity, gas, water, garbage, phone, internet, and cable.
- **Automobiles:** Buying or leasing your car(s), car insurance, gas, maintenance, and saving money for a new car.
- **Food:** Your groceries for you and your family, as well as any money spent on coffee and eating out.
- **Personal:** Your shopping (ex. clothing), hobbies, child care, health insurance, life insurance, medical co-pays, etc.
- **Debt**: Money you owe that isn't covered in other categories. These could include things such as student loans, credit cards, home equity line of credit (HELOC), and other loans.
- **Miscellaneous:** Other monthly expenses that you have which are not covered in the above categories.

Understanding Your Current Monthly Income

To begin, you need to have an understanding of how much money your household brings home each month (you plus your significant other if you have one). This is not the total amount of money that you make, but how much gets deposited in your personal checking account from each paycheck. If you are like most people, you have a rough idea of this number, but don't know for sure. So go through and make a list of the different monthly sources of income that your household brings in each month and the dollar amount.

Here are some potential sources of household income:

- Your paycheck from working a job
- Your spouse's paycheck from working a job
- Income from your business
- Income from your stock investments (ex. dividends)
- Child support and/or alimony
- Income from second jobs (ex. driving for a ride sharing service) or side hustles (ex. freelance website development)

Once you identify all your sources of income, write in the average amount of money that each source brings you in a month. You can typically get this information from your pay stubs or direct deposits into your bank account. Add all of the sources up and you will have your monthly cash flow in.

For example,

- Your Job: $4,500
- Your Spouse's Job: $2,000
  - Your Total Monthly Income: $6,500

Understanding Your Current Monthly Expenses

Now that you know your monthly income, the next step is to determine your monthly expenses. You likely have a handful of different categories that your expenses fall into. Start out by using the categories mentioned in the previous section. Gather up your bank statements from the last two months, along with any and all of your other bills. Spend a little bit of time going through them and categorizing your expenses into one of the above categories.

When finished, you should have all of your monthly expenses assigned to a category or subcategory and should have a total for each category (such as below):

- Pay Yourself First: $300
- Housing: $1,010
- Utilities: $510
- Automobiles: $1,000
- Food: $600
- Personal: $930
- Debt: $490

- Miscellaneous: $300
  - ○ Your Total Monthly Expenses: $5,140

Understanding Your Monthly Surplus/(Deficit)

Now that you know the sources and how much money comes in and goes out each month, you can figure out how much of a surplus or deficit you have each month. You will do this by taking your total monthly income and subtracting your total monthly expenses.

If you have more income than expenses, then you have a surplus and have more money coming in than your expenses. Congratulations! This is a great place to be!

If you have more expenses than income, that means that you have a deficit and are not bringing in enough income to cover your monthly expenses. You are either borrowing to pay your bills (either from your savings or from credit) or you are not paying your bills and are falling behind.

Using the example above, this is how you would calculate how much money is remaining.

- Your Total Monthly Income: $6,500
- Your Total Monthly Expenses: $5,140
  - ○ Your Total Monthly Surplus or (Deficit): $1,360 surplus/extra remaining each month

In this example, this couple is in a pretty good place. They have an extra $1,360 left over each month. This provides them some great flexibility and can be used to pay off debt (which we will cover in the next chapter) or be put into savings, which will make it easier to leave your job.

If you go through this activity and find yourself in a deficit, it can be a tough thing to come to terms with initially—but at least you know where you stand. That information will allow you to see where you can cut current expenses and explore additional ways to make more monthly income. If you need specific guidance on improving your personal finance situation, do a search online for Dave Ramsey and check out his book *The Total Money Makeover*.

Pay Off Debt

Debt is a major hurdle that prevents most people from achieving financial freedom and living the life that they want. In fact, we got into a lot of debt early on in our lives. Here is the breakdown of debt that we had accumulated by age 24:

- Student Loans: $66,000
- Credit Cards: $18,000
- Wedding Loan: $10,000
- Home Mortgage: $100,000
- Second Mortgage: $15,000
    - Total Debt: $209,000

So there we were. Twenty four year's old. Just married. And with $209,000 worth of debt!

If you don't currently have any debt (outside of say, your mortgage), congratulations! You have likely been very responsible with your money (or lucky) and can probably skip this chapter.

If you do currently have debt, as most people do, then this chapter is for you. As you can see, we've been where you are. In this chapter, we are going to share some of the best tips and strategies that we've come across that have helped us and others get out (and stay out) of debt. This is a *critical* piece of achieving the financial freedom and lifestyle that you desire.

Step 1 – Determine How Much Debt You Have

Your first step is figuring out how much debt you currently have and the sources of that debt.

You should have identified these sources of debt based on your monthly cash flow needs above. For each type of debt you have, go through and capture the following information:

- Type of debt & who it is owed to
- The remaining balance on the debt
- The interest rate
- The minimum monthly payment

With the following information identified, you can put this information into an organized table, such as the one shown below.

Creditor	Balance	Rate	Minimum Payment
Credit Card	$10,000	16.74%	$252
Auto Loan #1	$17,000	2.47%	$369
Auto Loan #2	$9,000	2.79%	$433
Student Loan	$20,000	4.5%	$237
Home Mortgage	$124,000	3.92%	$709
Totals:	**$180,000**		**$2,000**

Organizing your debts in this way will then let you see how much total debt, how much is owed on each debt as well as how much you are paying each month towards your debts.

In this case, we can see that $2,000 of this person's monthly budget is going towards his or her debt. That means that once this debt is paid off, this person will then not only no longer be in debt, but he or she will also have an extra $2,000 each month that he or she can allocate to building his or her ideal lifestyle.

Step 2 – Establish a Debt Payoff Strategy

Once you know how much debt you have, you may initially feel bad or overwhelmed. This is to be expected and is normal. (And you are not alone!) Even if you have more debt than you thought, knowing how much debt you have is powerful. It's the first step to owning your debt and not letting it own you.

Each of your debts has minimum payments, which is the minimum that you must pay on each debt each month without being charged additional fees. In our example, that's $2,000/month. This may initially not seem too bad until you look at how much it will cost and how long it will take to pay off all of your debts with just the minimum payments.

In the above example, the total debt is $180,000. If you only pay the minimum payments, it will end up costing you close to $250,000 total. That means that you will pay around $70,000 in interest on top of your $180,000. (Ouch!)

Oh—and it will take about 21 years to pay off, assuming you don't add any more debt on. That means if you are currently 35 years old, you won't have this debt paid off until you are around 56. (Double ouch!)

Clearly this is not the path that you want to take. So let's walk through some strategies and scenarios and help you plan out your course to get this debt paid off with a lot less money spent and in a much shorter time period.

The first strategy to help you pay off this debt faster is to pay extra money onto your debts beyond the minimum required. This can take years off of your payments and save you tens of thousands on interest.

The second that we recommend following is approach called the debt snowball. Dave Ramsey is a proponent of this method in his Total Money Makeover book that we mentioned above. It's a simple and effective strategy to help you tackle debt. Whereas traditional logic says that any extra money that you pay on your debt should go to the highest interest rate item (ex. a credit card with 20% interest), the debt snowball method says to apply it to the debt with the lowest balance (ex. a medical bill with a $500 balance).

Why would you do this, when simple math shows that you will pay more in interest with this method? The reason is simple; we often make emotional decisions, not logical decisions. Paying off your smallest loan first will give you a quicker win of having one of your debts paid off. You can see progress faster and start building momentum, as well as reduce the number of bills that you are paying each month. If you try to pay off a larger debt, you may only be making small dents, which can slow down your momentum and make you less excited (and committed) to paying off your debt. Plus, as an added bonus, you will then be able to take the money that you were paying towards that first debt and now add it to the payment of your next debt, which will help you pay that debt off even faster. This snowball effect really helps you build momentum and stick with it. See the impact in the table below when we combine the debt snowball with paying more than the minimum payments.

Total Debt	Monthly Debt Payment	Total Interest	Years to Pay Off
$180,000 (No snowball)	$2,000	~$70,000	21 Years
$180,000 (Debt snowball)	$2,000	~$35,000	9 Years
$180,000 (Debt snowball)	$2,500	~$27,000	6 Years
$180,000 (Debt snowball)	$3,000	~$21,500	5 Years

Note: When you download the Lifestyle Builders Starter Pack, you will get access to a calculator that will allow you to enter in your own numbers and run through these scenarios for you. You can get the starter pack at www. lifestylebuildersbook.com.

So after running a few scenarios, you can see the impact of increasing how much you are paying onto your debt each month and determine which amount and plan works best for your budget and your goals.

Now you may be thinking, "Tom and Ariana, this is great, but where am I going to find that extra money each month?"

Well, your first option is any money left over from your monthly budget above (your surplus). A second option is to look to reduce your monthly expenses. This can be done in a variety of ways, such as eating out less and reducing or canceling your cable. You can also start a low-cost side-business to generate some extra income that can be paid onto your debt, which we will be discussing in section 3 of this book.

There are lots of potential options. The key is really understanding that eliminating your debt is a key component to achieving financial freedom. Personal debt is an anchor and continuing to drag it around will slow your progress and make everything else much more difficult. Additionally, as we can see from this example, once your debt is paid off, you will free up hundreds or even thousands of dollars a month or more to spend in more exciting areas of your life.

Define Your Freedom Number

S o far, we've talked about budgets and debt. Boring, but necessary. When are we going to get to the fun stuff, like being able to quit your job?

Well, we are building towards that. Our next step is defining your *Freedom Number*. If you remember from earlier in this section, your Freedom Number is the amount of money that you will need each month in order to leave your job and be able to cover all of your expenses.

We know what you are thinking: "Didn't we already figure this out above when we defined our monthly cash flow needs/budget?"

We took the first step, but this is where most people fall short and end up hurting themselves when they leave their jobs. You see, when you leave your job, your monthly cash flow needs will change. Some of your expenses will increase while others decrease. We need to take those changes into account to figure out your Freedom Number.

Additional Expenses

First up, let's consider additional expenses that you will incur when you leave a job.

- **Health Insurance:** If you are getting your health insurance through your employer, you will need to use COBRA for a period of time (up to 18 months) or find and pay for your own health insurance. This can be costly. Prior to Tom leaving his job with health insurance, we were paying about $949/month for health insurance, which was the "Gold" plan.

This covered both of us and our 2 children. Our payment on this same plan if we used COBRA was ~$1,800/month. You heard that right. As a family of 4 living in New York, we would have to pay nearly $2,000/month ($24,000/year) just for health insurance. We did some shopping around and ended up with a "Bronze" high-deductible plan that "only" costs us $1,100/month.

Also, remember that your health insurance is typically a deduction BEFORE you get your paycheck. So you may not have included it in your monthly cash flow needs in step 1 above. Be sure to do some research on what your health insurance will cost after leaving your job and include it as an additional expense when calculating your Freedom Number.

- **Retirement:** Hopefully you are contributing to your retirement on a consistent basis. This can be done via a 401k, an IRA or some other means. Just like with your health insurance, this expense comes out before you see your paycheck, so be sure to add it to your monthly expenses when you leave your job. Also, remember that your employer may be matching your retirement contributions, so you will either be contributing less towards your retirement when you leave, or you will have to increase your monthly expenses to cover the additional retirement investment.

- **Self-Employment Tax:** Self-employment tax is actually the combination of two different taxes: FICA & Medicare. When you are employed, your company pays half of this while you pay the other half. Once you no longer work for another company, you will be responsible for the entire portion of this, which at the time of this writing is 15.3% (12.4% for Social Security tax and 2.9% for Medicaid tax). This is because you will continue paying your half, and your business will pay the other half.

- **Personal Income Tax:** This is what we all are used to paying. The specific percentages depend on many factors, but it starts at 10% and increases as your taxable income increases (capping out around 40%). Typically you will have money withheld from your paycheck to cover these taxes, again before you receive your money. So when you leave your job, you will need to include these costs into your monthly expenses and put this money aside.

- **State Income Tax:** Just like personal income tax, most states will impose a separate state income tax. We live in New York, so this is an additional 4-8.89% tax that needs to be accounted for. In total above, you can see that when you leave a job, you will owe a decent amount of the money that you earn in taxes (starting at 29.3% assuming the lowest bracket and living in New York).

- **Vacation:** While not an additional expense, you likely receive a vacation at your job (anywhere from 2-6 weeks depending on how long you've been employed). When you are an entrepreneur, you don't get any paid vacations unless you build them in. Especially during your first year in business, it's very likely that you may be working most or all 52 weeks of the year.

- **Sick Days:** Just like vacation, sick days are not an expense, but typically they are included in your work package. When you no longer have a job, if you need to take a sick day for you or your kids, that will be time that you are not working and potentially not getting paid.

- **Job Paid Perks:** Your company may offer perks that you will lose once you leave. For example, they may pay part of your phone bill or offer you access to the company gym. These perks will go away when you leave, so you will want to add them to your monthly budget.

Job-Related Savings

If you are adding things up as we go, you may think things look bleak. You probably just added a few thousand dollars to your monthly expenses when you leave your job, making it even more difficult to do so.

But don't stress. There are a handful of things that you can do to offset these additional expenses.

Costs That You No Longer Have

When you are working a job, you have certain costs that are directly related to that job.

- **Commuting Expenses:** It costs money to travel to work, such as gas for your vehicle. This could also be the cost of parking (depending on where you live) or the cost of public transportation. When you leave your job, you likely will no longer have these expenses. And if you do, they will likely be less and will be a tax deduction for your business. There are also some indirect savings! Since you won't be traveling as many miles, your car will have more resale value if you decide to sell or will give you more longevity.

- **Work-Related Meals/Coffee:** It can be so easy to spend money on food when you work a job. You don't feel like making lunch, you forget lunch, or a coworker wants to go out for lunch. This combined with stopping by your local coffee shop one or two times a week (or more) can really add up.

- **Work Clothing:** Your job may have a specific dress code. This dress code could require you to purchase clothing that you wouldn't purchase/wear otherwise. When you leave your job, depending on what business you have, you should be able to reduce or eliminate the money that you spent directly on work clothes (and work in pajamas if you're lucky!).

- **Miscellaneous Expenses:** Depending on your job and circumstances, you may be able to find other expenses that you save when you leave your job. For example, you might be paying for an increased data plan on your phone, but you may not need as much data if you will be working from home or can use the WiFi at your own business. Take a look at your budget and see if there are other expenses that you no longer need.

Downsizing Your Lifestyle

Although you can save some money on the items listed above, those items alone are likely not enough to make a significant impact on your monthly expenses. Another way to reduce your expenses and extend your runway (more on that later), is to downsize your lifestyle. This doesn't have to be a permanent downgrade, but any changes you make now will lower your expenses and make it easier to quit your job.

- **Downgrade Vehicles:** One option that can have a big impact on your expenses is to downgrade your vehicles. You may have vehicles that are more expensive than you need. If you own the vehicles outright, you may be able to sell them, buy a cheaper vehicle and put the difference into savings. If you are leasing or making car payments, you may be able to sell your vehicle and purchase a vehicle with lower monthly payments or even purchase a cheaper vehicle outright and eliminate monthly payments. Look for a car that is reliable and has low maintenance costs. You may even be able to get by selling one vehicle and sharing the other.

- **Downgrade Living:** Another option that can have a big impact on your monthly expenses is your living situation. You may have a house that is more expensive than you need or an apartment that is more than you need. If you have a house, you could sell the house and purchase a lower-cost house, move into a lower cost apartment, or even move in with a friend or family members. Your lower mortgage payments or lower rent will reduce how much money you need to make each month. You may also be able to make a profit if you sell your house, which can then go into savings.

- **Downgrade Insurance:** With a less expensive vehicle and/or less expensive house, you can likely reduce your insurance expenses on these items. Also, if you haven't already, you can typically get an additional discount by combining both policies under one insurance company.

- **Reduce Child Care:** If you are paying for your children to go to daycare 5 days a week, another option is to reduce the number of days that you kids attend daycare. If you are able to work with your kids home or can get everything done in 3 or 4 days, you can save some money on this expense. Be careful though. You may be better off continuing to have them in daycare so that you can focus on your work when they are there and being present with them afterward.

- **Reduce Cable:** Cable bills can easily run a few hundred dollars these days. You can scale back to a lower-cost plan, take advantage of a new member deal with another carrier, or drop it all together. Many people are "cutting the cord," meaning dropping cable and instead opting for services like Netflix, Hulu, and Amazon Video.

- **Reduce Subscription Services:** In addition to cable, review your monthly expenses and look for other subscription expenses that you can eliminate. You may have a gym membership that you never use, a music streaming service, or other subscriptions that you can cut. You may also be able to reduce some of your subscriptions, such as not needing as much data for your phone plan if you are working at home or in your office and can use Wi-Fi (as mentioned before).

- **Eat Out Less/Grocery Shop Smarter:** Most people spend a decent amount of money eating out every month, so you may be able to free up some budget there. You can eat out less, or swap out eating out for eating in. For example, maybe you enjoy a $5 frozen pizza instead of a $25 delivery on Friday night. You can also reduce/swap out some of the food on your grocery list. Sometimes switching to a different store can also save you money.

As you can see there are many different ways to reduce your expenses to ease leaving your job. Some may work for you, some may not. Some people like to go all in, drastically reduce expenses for the short term and give themselves more space to succeed. Others may want to take a more conservative approach, reducing some expenses to free up space, but not downgrade their cars or move in with a relative.

The important thing is discussing with your significant other and your family and decide what is the right decision for you. You might each have some things that are "on the table" and that you are OK with cutting back on, while others are "off the table" and things that you are not open to changing. It's important to lay items out together and come to an agreement that works for your specific circumstances. Cutting back some now can make it much easier to leave your job and achieve financial freedom.

But what if you want more than just leaving your job? What about all of the other things that you identified in the first section of this book? What about all the things that you wanted to have (like a bigger house, family vacations)? What about the experiences, the relationships, and the impact? Well, we define that as a different number, which we call your Dream Number.

You see, identifying your Freedom Number allows you to determine what you need to bring home every month to leave your job and design your life. The lower you Freedom Number is, the easier it is for you to achieve. As we just discussed, you can cut back on your lifestyle in order to lower your Freedom

Number, but you likely don't want to live this way forever. This is where your Dream Number comes in.

Your Dream Number is how much you need to bring home each month in order to have all of the things, experiences, relationships, and impact that you want. So step 1 would be to achieve your freedom, and step 2 would be to go after your dream and have everything that you want out of life.

To determine your Dream Number, go back to the vision that you created in chapter 1.2 where you defined the things, experiences, relationships, and impact that you want to have. Now you are going to go through a similar activity that you did when you defined your Freedom Number. Take a look at each item on that list and identify how much you need to bring home each month in order to have that. By doing this for each item on your list, you can then add each of these onto your Freedom number and you will get you Dream Number.

For example, let's say your Freedom Number is $5,000/month. As you look at your vision, you identify the following items that you don't need but wish you had/could do:

- Upgrade from a 2-bedroom to a 5-bedroom house
- Take family vacations 3 times a year

For each item on that list, do some research and determine how much money you need to bring home each month to cover that expense. Let's go through an example of this activity with a new house.

Let's say that you want to upgrade from a 2-bedroom to a 5-bedroom house. This home may cost $400,000 in the area where you want to live. You can take that number and plug it into a mortgage calculator and determine what your monthly payment would be. Let's say that you put 20% down ($80,000), you would need a mortgage for the balance of $320,000. Assuming you went with a 15-year mortgage at 4% interest, your monthly mortgage would be ~$2,400/month. (Note: We are using a 15-year mortgage here as that is the length that Dave Ramsey advocates for.)

Now with a house, you have some additional expenses that you will incur, such as taxes, insurance, and maintenance. So you will want to determine the additional costs of each of those as well. These numbers will vary by location, but let's say that your property taxes would be $12,000/year. That means that you need to bring home an additional $1,000/month to cover them. Your insurance may be $5,000/year, so you would need to bring home an extra $500/month to cover that expense. For maintenance, we will allocate 1% of the home's price for maintenance, or $4,000/year, which we'll round up to $350/month.

So in order to be able to move into your dream home, you need to bring home an additional $4,250/month. That's $2,400 to cover the mortgage, $1,000 to cover the taxes, $500 to cover the insurance and $350 to cover the maintenance.

Adding this amount to your Freedom Number of $5,000, you Dream Number becomes $9,250. Repeat this for each item on your vision board (including your vacation wishes and anything else that you dream to have) and you will end up with your overall Dream Number.

Chapter 2.5

What Size Business Do You Need?

One question that we often ask people is, "how much money do you need to bring in to leave your job?"

Most people get this number drastically wrong. This is for a variety of reasons:

- They don't truly know their monthly expenses
- They don't account for the additional costs they will incur when they leave their job

Now, if you've completed the activities from previous sections, then you should have a fairly accurate idea of your total monthly expenses. You have your Freedom Number defined and now have a clear target to shoot for. But there are still more scenarios lurking that can throw you off. For example: What type of business should you build that will allow you to achieve your Freedom Number?

Your first response may be, "A business that brings in $5,000/month." But that's not accurate. The money that you personally bring home (which goes into your PERSONAL checking account) is different than the money that your business brings in (which goes into your BUSINESS checking account). If you are treating the business money as your personal money, you are going to run into a whole plethora of issues, such as complicating the tracking of your personal and business finances, reducing your legal protection, and paying more in taxes.

Co-Mingling Funds

You are different than your business. Your name is different. Your age is different. You are identified differently by the government. In the US, your identity is tied to a Social Security Number (SSN), while your business's is tied to an Employer Identification Number (EIN).

Therefore, your money and your business's money are different. They should have separate checking accounts and your personal money should only be used for personal expenses while your business money should be used for business expenses. If you are mixing your personal and business money, then you are co-mingling your funds.

What does that mean? It means that you are mixing the two. Why is this a problem?

- Harder to Track Business Finances
  - If you can't accurately track money coming in and out of the business, you can't make decisions based on those numbers.
- Difficult to protect yourself (liability)
  - If someone were to sue you for anything in your business, and you have no separation between your personal and business finances, legally they can go after your personal money (even if you have an LLC).
- Paying more in taxes than required
  - When it comes time for you to file your taxes, not being able to identify your business expenses that can legally be deducted will cause you to miss these deductions and pay more in taxes than you are required.

Personal Income vs. Business Income

If you are not commingling funds, then you are treating your business income as separate from your personal income. This means that your personal income will be a *portion* of your business income. When you are an employee, you receive a paycheck, all of which you can spend on your personal expenses. Now when you are an entrepreneur, instead of just looking at your money through the lens of an employee collecting a paycheck, you also have to look at your money through the lens of the business.

So let's assume that your business made sales of the $3,500. That money would go into your *business* bank account, which is separate from your *personal* bank account. Now you need to begin deducting expenses from this *before* you pay yourself. The basic formula is:

Sales - Expenses = Profit

Sales are often sometimes called revenue. We need to take the money coming into the business and subtract the money going out of the business to determine how much profit the business itself makes. If we expand this formula a little bit, we can see that there are several things that we must remove before we figure out how much profit the business has made.

Sales - Cost of Goods Sold - Expenses - Taxes = Profit

In case you are not familiar with each of these terms, let's quickly define them.

- Sales: Money that the business brings in from selling products or services
- Cost of Goods Sold: Money required to create the product or service that the business is selling
- Expenses: Money required to run the business
- Taxes: Money that you owe the government

So let's place some numbers on each of these expenses to see what things look like.

Category	Amount	% of Sales
Sales	$3,500	--
Cost of Goods Sold	$700	20%
Expenses	$2,100	60%
Business Taxes	$280	8%
Profit	$420	12%

So what this means is that when the business makes $3,500, after all of the deductions come out, the profit remaining is only $420. Does this surprise you? Many business owners never go through this exercise and treat the $3,500 that comes into their business the same as the $3,500 that they get paid as an employee. This is a *huge mistake*. If you were to spend that $3,500 to pay your monthly bills, your business would run out of money and you would owe the government tax money that you now don't have—definitely landing you in debt, and possibly landing you in jail.

This is usually an eye-opening moment for most new business owners. They realize that the business typically has to make *more* money than they originally thought because they didn't factor in all of the additional expenses associated with running a business. Of course, one of the expenses is *paying yourself*. So you need to determine how much money they business needs to make in order for you to pay yourself your desired salary and allow the business to continue to grow. This has historically been a very tough thing to figure out, especially as a new business owner.

Introducing Profit First

If the last section confused or demoralized you, that's perfectly natural: you are starting to get a taste of what can easily happen if you don't treat your business like a business. So many new entrepreneurs just jump right into their business and never consider the true cost of doing business (as addressed above). They end up with a rude awakening later on after they spent a bunch of time and money on their business and end of having to close it because they are not making enough money. We are now going to show you a few simple strategies to model and design your business so you know exactly how much money it needs to make, and how that money should be split up, so that you can pay your business expenses, your taxes, and yourself.

In the previous section, we mentioned the basic way that businesses figure out how much profit they have, which is:

Sales - Expenses = Profit

As we also saw in that section, the various expenses from your business can eat up most or all of your profit if you let it. It's not uncommon for an entrepreneur to take no money from the business, or to calculate their hourly wage and have it well below minimum wage. We're thinking that you didn't decide to start your own business or make *less* than minimum wage, right?

You want to design your business—before you even start it—so that you have a clear understanding of what it needs to look like to achieve your personal goals. One of the main challenges that comes up when entrepreneurs attempt to do this is that it is then difficult to figure out exactly how much the business needs to sell in order for you as the owner to make the amount of money that you desire. Most entrepreneur just guess at this number, saying that they want to have a $5 million business, for example. But they have no idea if this is too much, too little, or just right. And if it's not the right number, they may end up building a business that they hate, because it doesn't allow them to do have what they want.

So before you proceed further, we want you to think about how big of a business you need. Yes, we want you to guess what size business you think you need to achieve your goals. Think about the number and write it down. In a little bit, we will come back to it.

Luckily, with a simple tweak to this formula, you can get a much better picture of what sort of business you need to build to achieve your Freedom and Dream Numbers. This tweak is to swap out expenses and profit. This gives us a new formula:

Sales - Profit = Expenses

This is exactly what Mike Michalowicz did in his book *Profit First: How to Transform Your Business from a Cash Eating Monster into a Money Making Machine.* This tweak may seem simple, but it makes a huge impact. Mike took the personal finance topic of "pay yourself first" that David Bach introduced in his book *The Automatic Millionaire*, and that we discussed in Chapter 2.2 and applied it to business. By defining and taking your profit first, you take chance out of the equation. You lock it in before that money goes anywhere else.

Along with many other great topics in the book, Mike introduces the concept of Target Allocation Percentages (TAP). This concept, seen below as a table, provides you some percentages to use when determining what percentage of your business sales/income goes into each category. You can use them as a guideline to design the business that you need.

Below is an example of what it looks like to use these Target Allocation Percentages in your business. Let's say that your business generates $100,000 in revenue over the course of a year. Below are the percentages and dollar amounts for how your money would be split into the various "buckets" according to the Target Allocation Percentages.

Bucket	%	Dollar Amount
Revenue	100%	$100,000
Profit	5%	$5,000
Owner's Compensation	50%	$50,000
Taxes	15%	$15,000
Operating Expenses	30%	$30,000

By breaking this out using this model, we can see that only 50% of your business income actually becomes your personal income. This means that not only do you actually pay yourself for the work that you do, but you make sure that it isn't too much that you don't have any money left over for business expenses and taxes.

So what does this mean for you? Because you know how much money you want to make (initially your Freedom Number, and eventually your Dream Number), it means that you can work backward to figure out how much money your business needs to make for this to become a reality.

So let's say for example that your Freedom Number is $5,000/month.

That means that the Owner's Compensation (your personal income) from your business is 50% of the business revenue.

So, in order to take home $5,000/month in Owner's Compensation, your business need to generate at least $10,000/month in Business income (basically double Owner's Compensation to determine business income).

Here's is a rough model of what your business would need to look like in that example.

Bucket	%	Annual Dollar Amount	Monthly Dollar Amount
Revenue	100%	$120,000	$10,000
Profit	5%	$6,000	$500
Owner's Compensation	50%	$60,000	$5,000
Taxes	15%	$18,000	$1,500
Operating Expenses	30%	$36,000	$3,000

Note: The Target Allocation Percentages vary based on how big your business is. For example, a business with less than $250,000 in revenue would use 50% for Owner's Compensation, while a business with revenue between $250,000 - $500,000 would be 35%. You can learn more about this by checking out the Target Allocation Percentages chart from Michalowicz's Profit First: How to Transform Your Business From a Cash Eating Monster into a Money Making Machine.

That means in order for this to work, you need to create a business that generates $10,000/month ($120,000/year). The expenses on this business cannot exceed $3,000/month ($36,000/year).

Your turn: Take your Freedom Number (which is monthly) and multiple it by 12 to see how much it is a year. Then see which range it falls into in the first column to then get an idea of the revenue range that you business would likely need. The above example assuming your Freedom Number was $10,000/month (so $120K/year), it could fall into Group A or Group B. If you then look at the Business Revenue Range for those 2 groups, that means you would likely need to build a business between $0 - $500K/year.

Group	Freedom Number Range (Year)	Business Revenue Range (Year)
A	$0 - $137.5K	$0 - $250K
B	$112.5K - $225K	$250K - $500K
C	$175K - $350K	$500K - $1M
D	$200K - $1M	$1M - $5M
E	$1M - $2M	$5M - $10M
F	$2M - $10M	$10M - $50M

> Note: This is not perfect math by any means, but it does give you an idea of how big of a business you would need to build to achieve your Freedom Number and Dream Number.

Now take the initial guess that you had for how much your business needed to make and compare it to the number that you just calculated. How do they compare? For most people, they often think that they need to build a bigger business than they need. For example, if you want a $10,000/month income, you likely don't need to build a $2 million business, but likely only a $500K business.

	Your Guess	Reality
How much revenue you think your business needs to generate a year?	$2M	$500K

Keep in mind that this quick calculation is not an exact science, but it does give you a starting point and a general idea. Depending on the specific business model that you choose (which we will cover in section 3 of this book), you may need to include some additional money into that calculation for purchasing the product that you sell, or your taxes may be different depending on where you are live or where run your business is located. The key is that most people have no idea what this number is initially. It might be a little more, it might be a little less, but you at least now have a ballpark number to guide you.

Chapter 2.6

Laying Out Your Runway

There is a common saying (which we hate), that says "entrepreneurs jump off the cliff and build the plane on the way down."

This is stupid—and is NOT how smart entrepreneurs build businesses.

Do you know why? Because when you jump off the cliff, you have a limited runway. That runway is the distance between the cliff and the ground. And we'll tell you, it is not very fun trying to build a plane while falling to Earth. That adds a lot of pressure onto you and ends with a very messy landing for most people (and often a crash).

Remember Wiley E. Coyote? What happened when he jumped off the cliff? He slammed into the earth and created a big hole. For entrepreneurs, this is a financial hole, as well as an emotional hole. And it is hard to dig your way out of it. You may have to go back to a job. You will probably blow through your savings. You will feel like you've failed, yourself and everyone around you.

Sure... you will hear the occasional "success story" of the entrepreneur who did this; they quit college or quit their job, had no business, minimal savings and made it all work (such as Mark Zuckerberg with Facebook). But for every person that falls into this criteria, there are *many* more who crash and burn. You just don't hear about them because they aren't exactly looking for attention.

We are not jumping off cliffs and building planes here; we are building a different runway. The runway you need is the number of months that you can

107

survive after leaving your job before you run out of money. Your runway is determined by 4 factors:

1. Your Freedom Number (monthly expenses after you leave a job)
2. Your personal income from your job
3. Your personal income from your business
4. Your savings that can be used towards your living expenses

So, what's the alternative to jumping off the cliff? Mapping out your runway horizontally (like airplanes) and giving yourself PLENTY of runway to gain speed and set yourself up for success before "taking the leap."

Before we discuss laying out your runway, let's describe some common scenarios that runways fall into:

Scenario #1: Your Personal Income (Owner's Compensation) from your business EXCEEDS your Freedom Number

Scenario #2: Your Personal Income (Owner's Compensation) from your business DOES NOT EXCEED your Freedom Number

The ideal scenario in this case is that the income that you are taking home from your business EXCEEDS your Freedom Number (Scenario #1). This means that you are working your job until this occurs, which could potentially be a while.

For example, if your Freedom Number is $5,000/month, then in the previous section you figured out that your business likely has to be bringing in more than $10,000/month.

This is ideal because once that happens, you can leave your job and you know that you have enough income coming in from your business to cover all of your monthly expenses without needing to tap into savings or go into debt to cover all of your expenses every month. In this scenario, your runway is *unlimited* as long as your business income stays above your Freedom Number. This is one way to reduce the risk of your plane (business) crashing because it runs out of runway. So if you can keep your job until you meet/exceed your Freedom Number from your job income, that is ideal.

With that said, most people don't want to wait this long and would prefer to leave their job sooner. In this case, they fall into Scenario #2 where their business income has not yet exceeded their Freedom Number. This means when they leave their job, they will be left with a gap between how much income they personally take home from their business and how much their monthly expenses are. This income gap will need to be covered by savings until the business income gets to a point where it equals or exceeds your Freedom Number.

Let's look at a few examples.

Example 1 - You Are Single

Freedom Number: $3,500/month

Job Income: $4,000/month

Business Income: $1,000/month

Savings: $5,000

Timeframe to leave your job: Three months.

Between now and when you leave your job, you would have $1,500 extra each month ($500 from your job and $1,000 from your business). This could be added to your savings for the next 3 months, allowing your savings to be $9,500 when you quit. At that point, your monthly expenses would be $3,500/month, but your business is only allowing you to take $1,000/month out (assuming that your business hasn't grown). This means that each month, in order to cover your expenses, you would need to use $1,000 from your business and $2,500 from your savings.

Your runway would be a little over three months. That means that once you quit your job, you would only have three months to get the money you pay yourself from your business to exceed your Freedom Number of $3,500. If you can't make that happen, you will run out of money and have to go back to a job.

If you can increase your business revenue by $200/month each month (increasing your Owner's Compensation by $100/month), you will extend your runway by one month (from three months to four months).

But if you can increase your business income by $600/month each month (increasing your Owner's Compensation by $300/month), you change from a three-month runway to a unlimited runway because your business income would exceed your expenses in ten months (seven months after leaving your job). You will have enough savings to get you through those first seven months. The chart below shows what this would look like monthly.

Month	Freedom Number	Income From Job	Income From Business	Surplus/ (Deficit)	Savings
Month 1	$3,500	$4,000	$1,000	$1,500	$6,500
Month 2	$3,500	$4.000	$1,300	$1,800	$8,300
Month 3 (Quit Job)	$3,500	$4,000	$1,600	$2,100	$10,400
Month 4	$3,500	$0	$1,900	($1,600)	$8,800
Month 5	$3,500	$0	$2,200	($1,300)	$7,500
Month 6	$3,500	$0	$2,500	($1,000)	$6,500
Month 7	$3,500	$0	$2,800	($700)	$5,800
Month 8	$3,500	$0	$3,100	($400)	$5,400
Month 9	$3,500	$0	$3,400	($100)	$5,300
Month 10	$3,500	$0	$3,700	$200	$5,500

Wow! So as we model this out, if you can increase your business revenue by $600 each month, you will actually set yourself up with an unlimited runway. This shows the power of understanding your runway as well as understanding how much more your business needs to sell in order to allow you to keep working on your business and not having to return to a job.

Example 2 - You and a Spouse are Both Working (and maybe have some kids)

Freedom #: $6,500

Your Income: $4,000/month

Spouse Income: $3,000/month

Business Income: $1,000/month

Savings: $1,000

Timeframe to leave your job: Six months.

With you leaving your job and your spouse staying in his or her job, you would only have around three months to increase your income from your business from $1,000/month to $6,500/month.

If you increase the business revenue by $200 each month, this would extend your runway to 7 months, and an increase of business revenue by $400 each month would give you an unlimited runway.

> *Note: We've created a spreadsheet to help you calculate your runway and have included it for you as part of the Lifestyle Builders Starter pack, which you can get at www.lifestylebuildersbook.com*

As you can see in these examples, different factors impact your runway. The longer you can keep your job, the more savings you build up and the faster you can increase your business income, the longer your runway is.

Also, none of these scenarios incorporate an emergency. You might have a house repair, car repair or other item that requires cash. Obviously, these would then tap into your savings and shorten your runway, so keep that in mind as you build these out.

So what key insights can we take from this?

- The longer you can stay with your job, the better position you put yourself in. This allows you to take financial pressure off your business (allowing you to make better business decisions), increase your savings and increase your business growth.
- When you do leave your job, the larger your savings, the longer your runway will be.
- Once you know how much you need to increase your business income each month, you will then be in a much better place to define your business goals and strategy. This allows you a better focus in your business.

So take some time and consider your various options and come up with a plan that works for you and your family. Be sure to have this discussion with your significant other (if you have one) and make sure you are on the same page (as we learned from our experience, if you're not on the same page it can create a huge block in creating your runway).

With your plan in place, the next step is to work your plan. This means focusing on the following areas:

- Excelling at your current job to keep that income coming in while you work on your plan.

- Set, stick to and review your budget each month.
- If you have debt, follow the debt payoff plan that you created.
- Use the additional money that you have left each month to build up your savings.
- If you have a business, focus on increasing your business revenue to allow you to bring home more income from your business.
- If you don't have a business, go through the process of brainstorming different business ideas. The initial steps for this are covered in the next section of this book (Concept to Cash).

As with anything, the plan that you create sounds great when you create it, but chances are it will not go as smoothly as you anticipate. Things will come up that throw it off. Some of your assumptions may be incorrect. Whatever the reason, a *critical* piece of making this entire thing work is checking in on your progress and making adjustments. Luckily, you're prepared to track your progress towards your goals and have a framework to check in (Chapter 1.6). So where does this financial check-in occur? The most critical check-in time that we recommend is your monthly meeting.

Why monthly? It allows you enough time to gather empirical data while not waiting too long to act on it or recalibrate. Additionally, it is good practice to put together your monthly cash flow plan (budget) as we defined in Step 1. Monthly you can check in and see how you actually did compared to the plan and make adjustments, either to the plan or to your budget, for the upcoming month.

If you have a significant other, this is also a great time to discuss any changes and remain in sync.

Lifestyle Builder Starter Pack Resource
These Worksheets and Guided Activities will help you work through some of the numbers and things we walk through in this section. This is included with your starter pack that you get for free with this book. Get your free copy at www.lifestylebuildersbook.com

Section 3:
Concept to Cash

Section Summary:

Once you know what it looks like you achieve financial freedom, your next course of action is to create a business that will enable you to achieve that financial freedom. Most people go about this process backward: They create the product or service first, then attempt to sell it. This section of the book shows you a better way, including how to brainstorm ideas, narrow down and select one, test and tweak the concept and start making money.

Chapter 3.1

A "Great Idea" Can Cost You A Lot

Tom's Take

After we purchased our first investment property, I was hooked! After putting in the upfront work to buy and do some renovations, we were now making extra money every month without a lot of additional effort. We continued to purchase more properties, and with each property, we were one step closer to replacing Ariana's income and allowing her to stay home when we eventually would start having kids. We had both been working hard during the previous few years. We both had jobs, and I was spending at least one if not both days on the weekend driving to our investment properties and renovating them. It was tough work and long days, but I was learning a lot and we were moving towards our dreams. Even though we were working a lot, we still made sure to carve out some time for each other and for our individual hobbies, which were video games for me and reading for her. We did this by making sure we scheduled time for these activities on our calendars.

Four year after that first investment, Ariana became pregnant. It was one of the happiest moments of my life. It also came with some worry and concern. I knew nothing about being a father, and instead of just worrying about the two of us, we would now have to figure out what our lives looked like with a baby in the mix.

We were at the point where Ariana would be able to stay home when our first child was born, which was the plan. Then the next step was to replace my income and get me home. Over each of the prior years, I had steadily increased my day-job salary. While this was great, it also meant that it would now take more

115

investment properties in order to replace my income and allow me to leave my job. So as excited as I was for this next phase in our life, I was also starting to feel anxious and a little concerned about me being able to retire by age 35. This would require purchasing many more investment properties, and I was concerned about my ability to keep up with everything. I knew I wouldn't be able to—and didn't want to—spend all of my weekends renovating houses when our daughter was born. I needed to rethink my plan.

One Saturday after tearing out drywall from one of our newest investment properties, my father and I took a break to grab lunch at a local pizzeria. While eating, I heard someone mention that there was a wine and liquor store for sale in the neighboring town where all of our real estate was located. Years before, I had actually helped my father purchase a wine and liquor store and retire early from his job, so this caught my attention as opportunity for me to explore! If I could replicate what I did for my father and have similar success, I could leave my job. So, we finished up our work, and I drove home excitedly and declared to Ariana, "We are buying a liquor store!"

As usual, she began to tell me all the reasons it was a bad idea. But just like real estate investing, I was convinced this was the right move because I took my father through the process and knew the earning potential for a store like this. I knew it was just a matter of time until I got her on board. Unlike when I started the real estate business, this time I had learned a little and we sat down and discussed this opportunity. Ariana made a pros and cons list, as she usually does. We didn't have our goal-planning process perfected yet, but we did have an initial roadmap of what we wanted our lives to look like. So, after looking at the pros and cons list as well as our goals, we jointly decided that we would look into buying the store.

With Ariana's blessing, I was off to the races. I began doing my research, only to quickly find all sorts of problems with this plan. The location of the store was terrible. The store was small and wouldn't allow for growth. And the owner was asking far too much money. I was frustrated. I had reflections back to the initial roadblocks that I encountered when starting the real estate business. But as any successful person does, I didn't give up and kept searching for a solution. And then it hit me: We already owned the real estate business, why don't we just purchase a building and open our own store? And that is what we did.

Part of opening this new business was seeing opportunity and getting excited. Part of it was also diversifying our income. We started our real estate business in 2008, right after a large majority of people had lost a lot of money in real estate. Even though we were going about it in a smart way, part of me wanted to diversify our income into something that wouldn't be directly impacted by the real estate market and the economy (the alcohol business is known to be pretty recession resilient).

So, I got knee deep into putting a business plan together, weaving it in between the hours of my grad school classes (working toward my Masters in Business Management). I had 3-hour classes several nights a week, as I wanted to finish school before our daughter was born. I would often wake up at 2 or 3 a.m. and work on it for a few hours before heading off to my day job and then to class at night. I didn't see Ariana much during this time.

I had loosely written a business plan for the real estate business, but I knew a retail-store business plan would need to be much more comprehensive. I spent several weeks working on it, piecing different information on how to write a business plan together from various sources. Even though I was in grad school for business management, most of the concepts were geared towards running existing businesses, not starting new ones.

I projected startup costs for this business at $39,050. I also projected out sales and expenses for three years—a strategy I learned from my research on business planning. According to the plan, we would go from selling $130,000 in year one up to $182,000 in year three.

We would also go from making $21,000 in profit the first year to $61,664 by year three. At the time, my corporate job as a software developer was bringing me in ~$68,000/year. So according to the plan, we should nearly replace it within three years. At the time I was twenty-seven years old, so that would be five years earlier than planned. (Sweet!)

> *Before we go any further, let me just say that I wish I had known about and had gone through the activities in section 2, specifically the financial analysis of the business where I took sales - cost of goods sold - operating expenses - taxes = profit. And I wish I would've asked for some help with this analysis, as it would've helped us avoid a lot of challenges.*

So how did we do? Oh, if only the real world worked the same way my twenty-something brain did.

Our first full year in business (2013), we sold $149,311.09. Sweet! We made $19,311.09 more than planned! So, our cash flow (profit) should be much higher than $21,644 that I estimated in year one, right?

Wrong. Dead wrong. We lost about $17,712 the first year. That's a $39,376 swing from our planned profit of $21,664. Ouch.

So, what went wrong?

- **Inventory:** By far the biggest miss was with how much we would spend on inventory. When you sell a product or service, you will spend a certain amount of money to purchase or build that product/service (as you now know is Costs of Goods Sold). According to the initial plan, about 23% of the money that we made ($30,000) would go back into inventory. The reality is that we ended up spending 69% on inventory that first year. That means instead of spending $30,000/year, we spent $102,160 on inventory. Therefore, we only had $46,353 remaining to cover the rest of the business expenses.

- **Operating Expenses:** Whenever you estimate your expenses, you will be wrong. Your expenses will be much higher than you initially anticipate, and this was true for us in the first year. There were many expenses that I hadn't anticipated, such as the $1,000 shipping cost of the shelving and the $3,500 fine when one of our employees accidentally misread someone's birth date and sold alcohol to someone underage, among many others. These fees came out of our personal funds as we did not have any money saved up for emergencies.

- **Taxes:** I didn't understand how much we would owe in taxes, and when we would owe them. We opened the store in November, right before the busiest time of the year. I knew that we would need to pay taxes, but my timing was off. So, we ended up having to pay more taxes than I had anticipated (and a month earlier than I had planned). This resulted in Ariana and I personally having to put another $4,000 into the business to cover the taxes.

So my "great idea" for a business lost $17,712 in year one. We didn't give up, though. And with a few adjustments, we earned a $29,000 profit in our fifth full year in business, which is about an 11% Return on Investment (ROI). Looking at the target allocation percentages from Profit First, the recommended profit for this size business is 10%, so we are right in line. That just goes to show you the difference between your hopefulness in the business plan and what a financial projection tells you and the reality once you open the business. If only we had found the Profit First method before we opened the store!

I wish I could tell you that this was our only business blunder, but that is far from the truth. We've had other ideas that we thought were great (correction, that *I* thought were great). For example, after we started both the real estate investing business and the wine/liquor store (along with several others that failed), we had people start asking us how to start a business. We had clearly made a bunch of mistakes along the way and had learned some valuable lessons, so we figured that we had some valuable information to share and could help others. And as always, the entrepreneur in me is looking for the next opportunity to not only make money, but to make an impact.

After listening to some podcasts and getting inspired, I decided that we were going to launch a $500 course called "30 Days to Launch," showing people (specifically couples) how to launch a business in 30 days. We spent about $1,000 on equipment (camera, microphones, a green screen, etc.) We planned everything out. We created 30 worksheets. We recorded 30 videos. We did it all. We were so excited for the launch. After one month available to the public, we generated a total of—wait for it—2 sales. You read that right. Those two sales brought us in a grand total of $94. (And I'm pretty sure one sale was friend who felt bad for us.) We earned a grand total profit of -$906.

Just like the liquor store, I started this business when Ariana was 8 months pregnant with our son. Apparently, this is my version of nesting. Ariana gets the house ready for the baby and I start a new business.

We have many more failures than this. In fact, we had so many failed businesses or products that at one point we did a podcast episode called "Our Business Graveyard: Dedicated to Those Businesses No Longer With Us."

Successful businesses come after many tweaks and pivots. More often than not, the final product offers little resemblance to the original idea. For example, Twitter originally came out of a company called Odeo, which was a podcasting platform[3]. Another example is 3M, which originally started as a mining company[4]. Many companies go through these shifts. They find issues with the original idea and keep changing/tweaking it until they find a business model that works.

So, what did we do after launching "30 Days to Launch"? We (I) had the next great idea. Instead of a 30-day standalone program, we would launch a full-on course, taking people all the way through the process of creating a successful business. In reality, we used the base concepts of "30 Days to Launch" and expanded on them. We also better organized it by getting feedback from people who we were building this form and creating a more step-by-step process to take them to their desired outcome.

Ariana's Take

I'll take over from here, as Tom did a great job of walking through how all of his "great ideas" either failed or lost us money. And losing money is exactly what you want when you're about to have a baby, right? (Twice.) I'd like to officially nominate him for #dadoftheyear and #husbandoftheyear.

> *(Of course, I'm adding those hashtags jokingly. Please really take some time to think and plan before you start a business while you are working on starting or expanding your family. It will ultimately add a multitude of challenges and difficulties into your life, just when you should be working to take things off your plate and simplify. The best thing you can do for your relationship and your family is to give yourself the space and time to enjoy adding a new member to your family. That being said, I know opportunities happen and we can't always control the timing! I just want to share from experience that dealing with the extra stressors really put a strain on us at an important time in our lives.)*

As Tom mentioned, the year we were to become parents for the first time was the year we started our liquor store! That is also the year I left my job, so while I was able to stay home and care for our newborn daughter, I also stepped into the role of manager for both the real estate business and the store. (While this was not a part of the original plan, me taking on these roles allowed the businesses to continue running smoothly as Tom was still working his full-time job.) I'd had no experience running either, and oh boy did we learn a lot along the way! I remember thinking "I wish there were a manual I could reference for how to do all of this stuff!"

We had the Internet, of course. But many things were pushed along by pure determination and grit. These businesses COULD NOT fail, we had too much riding on them!

And so, we managed. Neither of the businesses were where we wanted them to be yet, but they were staying afloat, and we had high hopes for their growth and long-term gains. (Plus, how cool is it to get free alcohol?! Our family and friends certainly liked the perks.)

About one year in we started getting requests to help other people get their business started—and we helped several people. For example, we helped our aunt put her business model together for personal training business, allowing her to grow from a side business in her garage to a full-on personal training business in a professional facility (GAME Training represent!)

Tom decided we'd make this a legit thing. We brainstormed a name: Entreprenewlyweds. We were entrepreneurs, and started our first business when we were newlyweds, so why not just smash them together to create the business name? We had a great message and a great idea, but we quickly learned that we lacked a clear business message. No one knew who the company served or what the heck the company did. (Worse yet, we learned a clever name isn't such a good idea if no one can spell it!) When the "30 Days to Launch" product flopped, we decided to start from scratch—create a new name, start a new podcast, go to our first in-person conference together, the whole nine yards. (By this time, we'd had our son. Somehow Tom convinced me I *had* to be at this event, and we left our exclusively breastfed 4-month-old with my parents for four very long days.)

That is when we shifted away from Entreprenewlyweds and started *Serial Startups*. We were serial entrepreneurs, and we wanted to help people build multiple streams of income!

We got our dreams crushed a bit. The entrepreneurs hosting the event–two couples who had each started and grown successful online businesses–told us straight up our plan needed some tweaking, and although it felt a bit defeating, we persevered. Their advice was to stick to the brick & mortar space, since that is what we had done, that was what we knew best, right? That we needed to "niche down" instead of trying to help everybody everywhere. They didn't know what they were talking about! Our idea was great! (Read those with sarcasm and a shake of the head). So, on we went to continue the podcast and to launch a training and membership site online called Startup Academy.

We had *amazing* content thanks to Tom. He had taken all of his experience—from his corporate jobs, his business consulting work, his degrees, and our business experience—and pulled it together and built out an arsenal of training materials and videos. We had a whole framework worked out, people would follow the "Startup Roadmap" and we would help them take their idea from start to success! And we even had a good group of founding members who joined, more than the two people who bought "30 Days to Launch."

And then it stalled. We couldn't get more people to sign up. Members were leaving. Something was off. Maybe the hosts of that conference had been right in some ways, saying that we needed to niche down and hone in our messaging. No way! We had two successful businesses: We must know what we were doing.

It took me having a mini meltdown for us to go back to the drawing board. I didn't love our Serial Startups brand. I didn't feel connected to the 1,300 people we had in a free community built around the brand. I remember sitting in our home theater, on our "comfy couch" (a $20 steal from a roommate in college, with the most hideous 70s style fabric), crying. Tom asked me, point blank: "Do you want to just stop all of this? Do we need to do something else?"

To be honest, I entertained that idea for several minutes. I remember thinking how much easier everything would be if we went back to normal jobs and didn't have the stress of running three businesses. No more annoying tenants, no more emergency late-night trips to clean a flooded basement at the liquor store. No more feeling out of my comfort zone trying to help other people in the business world.

Though if we did go back to our normal jobs, we'd sacrifice our main objective: To retire by age 35. The work was hard, but the goal was too important to us to abandon. That talk was the catalyst for everything that is now happening in our business and life. Our idea was solid, but our message and the people we wanted to help hadn't been crystal clear. This is such a common problem for people when they try to start a business, and we were no exception to that rule.

I wanted to help people like *us*—people who were trying to build their business to create a better life for their loved ones! Spouses who wanted more freedom and choice in how they lived with their partner. Parents who wanted to be present and get time back with their kids. I remember sitting in the car with Tom one day while we were waiting to meet with our accountant. We started brain dumping who we wanted to work with, what we stood for, and what we stood against. From that, we crafted our manifesto (which you can read at lifestylebuildersbook. com). It was that manifesto that helped us clarify who we wanted to help and how we wanted to help them.

We re-branded our business and free community from "Serial Startups" to "The Family Entrepreneur Life Community" and the response was astounding! People loved the concept. It was a place we could all congregate together, free of judgement, and talk about business and life all in one.

And after some time, we started to see a need, to hear some themes in the group. I dug into market research and we got on calls with more than 50 entrepreneurs in our network. What were *they* struggling with? What did *they* already try to solve that problem? Why didn't it work? What could we offer that would solve their struggles? How could we help them build the right business for their life goals?

It was like a beautiful break in the clouds after a storm. After talking to all these entrepreneurs with families, we realized that they were creating their businesses for the same reasons we were—to build our ideal lifestyles. So Lifestyle Builders™ was created, with the tagline:

Your Life. Your Business. Your Way. ™

Everything fit right into place. *This* was what we were meant to be doing all along. These were the people we could impact the most, and we wanted to! The few Startup Academy members we had remaining transitioned over, and we started off Lifestyle Builders™ with a bang and 20 new members with the initial soft launch.

Chapter 3.2

Idea Brainstorming

All new businesses start with an idea. You may already have an idea for your business, or you may still be searching. Either way, we recommend going through the brainstorming process. As you read in our story that kicked off this section, many businesses end up looking very different by the time they find success from when they were first started. Your goal is to get as many potential ideas on the table as possible. By going through this process, you will have a big list of potential winners to evaluate and choose from, giving you the highest chance of success.

The Brainstorming Process

Brainstorming is a pretty straightforward process, but here are a few guidelines to help you be most effective with the process.

Our favorite tools for brainstorming are Post-It Notes. They are simple, cheap, easy to create, and easy to toss in the recycle bin. You could use a piece of software, but nothing beats the ease and simplicity of Post-It Notes. Often times finding the "perfect" tool can delay the brainstorming process as you search for it, sign up for it, and try to figure out how to use it. Do you remember back in section 1 where we discussed keeping things simple and focusing on effectiveness? That's why you will always hear us recommend Post-It Notes, paper, or a whiteboard.

Here are some guidelines to follow as you go through the process:

- Let the ideas flow. Resist the urge to judge or filter them. Just get all the ideas out of your head and go through them after.
- You can brainstorm alone but going through the activity with another

person or a small group will generate more ideas and you can often build off each other's ideas.

- After you get all of the ideas out of your head, you can then organize, prioritize, and eliminate them.
- At the end of this process, you want to whittle down your big list of ideas into a smaller list of 5-10 ideas that you can take into the next step.

So get your post it notes out and let's run through the brainstorming process by going through several activities. For each activity, ask yourself the following questions and write your answers down on Post-It Notes. The goal of this activity is to generate a large list of ideas for you to choose from.

Brainstorming Activity #1: Looking in the Mirror

The first source for business ideas comes from you. So, in this activity, you will take a look at yourself and ask the following questions:

- What interests, hobbies, and passions do you have?
- What things do people come to you for advice on?
- What struggles/challenges do you face or have your overcome?
- What strengths or weaknesses do you have?
- What's your unfair advantage?

The focus here is on your experience.

Brainstorming Activity #2: Looking at the Industry

Take a look at the industry that you have experience in. Ask yourself these questions:

- What gaps exist in your industry?
- What do customers complain about?
- What trends are going on, both in your industry and in general?
- What can you maximize or minimize to serve a different need?
- What hasn't changed over the past 10 years?

The focus here is on an industry.

Brainstorming Activity #3: Looking at Customers

Look at the people that you want to work with and serve:

- What types of people do you enjoy working with?
- Who do you want to help?
- What problems or challenges does this group face?
- What do they seek/enjoy?

The focus here is on people.

Brainstorming Activity #4: Looking at Innovation

Look at what already exists and see how you can change/innovate it:

- What two products or services could be combined to create a new product or service?
- What can you eliminate from a product to make it better?
- Challenge current boundaries. Ask "What if"?

The focus here is something new.

Brainstorming Activity #5: Looking at Cloning

Look at what is already working somewhere else and apply it to you space.

- What existing business can work in a different market or space?
- What ideas exist in one industry that can be applied to another?

The focus here is transferring already working ideas.

After spending some time going through these questions, you will likely have a decent list of potential ideas that could become businesses.

Narrowing Down Ideas

After going through the above activities, you should have a pretty comprehensive list of ideas for potential businesses that you could start. The next step is to then prioritize these ideas and decide which one will be the first that you will focus on testing out.

For a long time, we struggled with figuring out the best way to do this. Then we came across a concept that made it so simple: Ikigai.

Pronounced i-kai-gai, it is a Japanese concept that means "reason for being."

Now this may seem like a weird way to narrow down business ideas but bear with us: You already know that you should be building your business to reach your Freedom Number that helps you live your ideal life. Given that

Ikigai means your reason for being, it is a great way to help determine the right business for you.

Ikigai has four main parts:

- What You Love
- What You Are Good At
- What The World Needs
- What You Can Get Paid For

And with that simple breakdown, you can figure out your reason for being.

If you look at what you love and what you are good at, that is your *PASSION*.

If you look at what you are good at and what you can be paid for, that is your *PROFESSION*.

If you look what you love and what the world needs, that is your *MISSION*.

And if you look at what the world needs and what you can be paid for, that is your *VOCATION*.

IKIGAI

1. DELIGHT AND FULLNESS, BUT NO WEALTH
2. EXCITEMENT AND COMPLACENCY, BUT SENSE OF UNCERTAINTY
3. COMFORTABLE, BUT FEELING OF EMPTINESS
4. SATISFACTION, BUT FEELING OF USEFULNESS

The Concept of Ikigai.
Adapted from TheStar.com, by Toronto Star, 2016,
Retrieved from https://www.thestar.com/life/relationships/2016/09/06/
why-north-americans-should-consider-dumping-age-old-retirement-pasricha.html.
Copyright Toronto Star Newspapers Ltd. 1996 -`2019

So, the ideal is to find a business that checks each of the four boxes above. When entrepreneurs are struggling, usually the business that they are trying to build doesn't check all of the boxes.

For example, when people ask what business they should start, people will often respond with "do what you love" or "follow your passion." That is just one of the boxes, and those who follow this advice often run into issues when they don't determine how the world needs what they love (and if they need it enough to pay for it). This is why most "entrepreneurs" end up with an expensive, time-consuming hobby, that generates very little money for them. They are doing what they love but haven't figured out how to get people to pay them for it. If you love eating pizza, that could be an expensive hobby, until you can answer the other questions above.

So we use the four above criteria to help prioritize and decide which plan to test, but we also add in one additional criteria: how well does this business idea align with your personal vision and goals. As we discussed previously, whatever business you decide to create, in addition to serving your customers, that business should then also serve you and help you achieve your ideal life and happiness.

Filling out a simple table like this will help. Give each idea that you have a rating. One means it doesn't do well in that category, while five means it does very well. For example:

Idea	Love	Good At	Need	Pay For	Alignment	Total
Idea 1	5	5	3	4	5	22
Idea 2	4	3	3	4	2	16
...						

After going through this activity, you'll add up the scores to determine your top five ideas. Select those and continue on.

The One-Page Business Plan

What's the first step in starting a business? Creating a business plan, of course!

We've written so many business plans over the years. If someone would read through them, you would think that every idea for a business was a home run. You saw an example of this in the introduction to this chapter when we discussed our wine and liquor store. Reality was *very* different than what we initially described in the plan.

But here is the reality of traditional business plans:

- They are boring.
- They are tough to create.
- They are often wrong.
- They often don't get used after they are done.

Traditional business plans are often many pages of vague explanations and fancy business jargon. No one really enjoys writing them, and most times they are only created to show to a bank or private investors for a business loan. Filled with projections and guesses on the hoped-for outcomes, these plans very seldom come to full fruition, and therefore make it hard to follow them once created. It can also be difficult to update them, so most end up sitting on the shelf collecting dust, offering little ongoing value.

So, does that mean that you shouldn't do a business plan? Heck no!

What it does mean is that you should adopt one of the more modern approaches to business planning, which not only can be done much faster, but is also a much more enjoyable and engaging way to get your business started—and guide you as it grows.

From Business Plan to Lean Canvas

In 2008, Alexander Osterwalder created the Business Model Canvas. This was a stark contrast to what came before, which were the 30-plus-page traditional business plans. He outlined not only the Business Model Canvas, but also the process for creating and utilizing it in his book, *Business Model Generation*. He took the business plan down to a single sheet.

But what is a business model and how does it differ from a business plan? In the book, Osterwalder offers us a simple yet effective definition of a business model:

> *"A business model describes the rationale of how an organization creates, delivers, and captures value."*

This is powerful. In our experiences, most struggling or failed businesses can't get all three aspects listed in the definition right. They may not have a valuable product or service—and if they do, they may not know how to consistently deliver that value to the right people. If they have a valuable offer *and* can deliver it to the right people, they fail to properly capture the value that they have created and delivered into a profitable business.

Since the creation of the Business Model Canvas, several variations have been created. One spinoff—which is very effective for new business ideas—is the Lean Canvas, created by Ash Maurya. Given that we were looking for something better suited for startups and new businesses, we decided to check it out.

> *"My main objective with Lean Canvas was making it as **actionable** as possible while staying **entrepreneur-focused**. The metaphor I had in mind was that of a grounds-up tactical plan or blueprint that guided the entrepreneur as they navigated their way from ideation to building a successful startup....*
>
> *My approach to making the canvas actionable was capturing that which was most uncertain, or more accurately, **that which was most risky**."* [5]

As you have probably heard, from your mom to your co-workers to everyone who isn't actually an entrepreneur, most new businesses fail within the first 5 years. While some sources have provided statistics to support this over the years, more recent studies give less of a black and white answer. Regardless, you've probably heard "business is risky, you should just stick with your secure job" from the same group of people. Well guess what, everything has risk. You could arrive at your "secure" job tomorrow, only to find that your company was sold, and they are laying off your department. On the drive home, you could get hit by a bus that places you in the hospital, limiting your ability to look for a new job (or much, much worse). Telling your spouse that you want both of you to retire by age 35 has risks (but is *totally* worth it). Risk is all around us. It's how you *prepare* for the risk, that separates successful entrepreneurs and those still trying to break through.

The key is not to let risks stop you from proceeding forward, but to identify the risks, and then systematically work on reducing the risks. Whereas people often believe that entrepreneurs are risky humans, in my experience, most successful entrepreneurs actually focus on *mitigating* risk—minimalizing it. Many entrepreneurs who fail are the ones who didn't take the time to identify and reduce/remove the risk, and ultimately moved forward with their business that was set up to fail from the beginning.

Successful entrepreneurs, on the other hand, are the ones who focused initially on defining and mitigating this risk and made adjustments based on what they learn. You see, a business idea that you come up with is really just your guess (or hypothesis) of what will work. Without testing it, you will likely overlook glaring assumptions that turn out to be incorrect. So instead, once you take your assumptions out of your head and put them on paper, your next step is then to test each assumption.

This is what the Lean Canvas and Ash's corresponding book, *Running Lean: Iterate From Plan A to a Plan That Works*, is all about. The canvas fits on a single page and highlights the nine key areas that entrepreneurs should work through with a new idea:

- **Customer Segments** - The customers who you plan to serve
- **Problem** - The top three problems that the customer segments have
- **Unique Value Proposition** - A single, clear, and compelling message that states why you are different and worth buying
- **Solution** - The top three features to solve the top three problems
- **(Marketing) Channels** - The path to your customers

- **Revenue Streams** - Basic financial information for how you will make money
- **Cost Structure** - Basic financial information for your business expenses
- **Key Metrics** - The key activities that you measure to show forward momentum
- **Unfair Advantage** - What do you have that can't be easily copied or bought

LEAN CANVAS

PROBLEM	SOLUTION	UNIQUE VALUE PROPOSITION	UNFAIR ADVANTAGE	CUSTOMER SEGMENTS
1	4	3	9	2
	KEY METRICS		CHANNELS	
EXISTING ALTERNATIVES	8	HIGH-LEVEL CONCEPT	5	EARLY ADOPTERS
COST STRUCTURE	7	BREAK-EVEN	6	REVENUE STREAMS

Lean Canvas with numbered boxes.
Adapted from Lean Stack, by A. Maurya, 2012,
Retrieved from https://blog.leanstack.com/why-lean-canvas-vs-business-model-canvas.
Copyright 2012 by LEANSTACK.

By sitting down and filling out this information, you will have the initial assumptions for your business idea laid out in an organized way. This will allow you to begin testing all of your assumptions.

Now it's time to pick the first idea to fill out your canvas.

Idea Selection

Heading back to your list of ideas, you should now have it initially narrowed down using the five criteria:

- What You Love
- What You Are Good At
- What The World Needs
- What You Can Get Paid For
- Alignment to your personal vision/goals

What we want to do with this step is to take the top three ideas and fill out a Lean Canvas for each of them. Allocate between 30-60 minutes to complete each Lean Canvas. This should provide you with enough time to get your basic idea and assumptions out on paper, but not take too much time that you put off actually doing it or trying to go into too much detail. For example:

Once you have your three Lean Canvases filled out, you will work on scoring each idea to learn which one has the best chance of becoming a successful business for you. To do this, you will go through a similar ranking activity as before. For each canvas, you will rank the 10 boxes on a scale of one to five. Giving a category a ranking of one means that it isn't that great, three being that it is OK, and five being that it is great. At the end, you will be able to add up the numbers and see which idea you should move forward with to validate.

1	2	3	4	5
Strongly Disagree	Disagree	Neutral	Agree	Strongly Agree

Box 1 - Customer Segment
- Is your customer segment big enough to build a business around? Is it niched/narrowed down enough to allow you to speak specifically to a person/small group within it?

Box 2 - Problem
- Are the problems identified big enough/important enough? Are the customers from Box 1 likely to pay what you desire to solve the problem?

Box 3 - Unique Value Proposition
- Is what you plan to offer different enough from existing products or services so people will choose you over your competition?

Box 4 - Solutions
- How feasible does your solution seem? Will you be able to implement it yourself or will you need help from others?

Box 5 - Channels
- How easy is it to find these customers? Do the congregate in specific places? Do you already have some of them in your current network that you could speak to?

Box 6 - Revenue Streams
- Are you able to charge a premium? Does the customer segment have enough money/is likely to pay what you want for the solutions?

Box 7 - Cost Structure
- Is it going to cost a lot to create this initial offer? Do you have the money or the ability to get the money required to start and run this business?

Box 7.5 - Breakeven
- Do you need a few dozen customers to break even? A thousand?? How easy/difficult will it be to get to break even?

Box 8 - Metrics
- How difficult will it be to capture and track these key metrics? Can they be automated, or will they need to be tracked manually?

Box 9 - Unfair Advantage

- How solid is your unfair advantage? Will it allow you to beat out a competitor that is using the same business model?

When you have gone through and ranked each box on your Lean Canvas, add them up. Your highest possible score is 50 (each of the 10 questions above can have a max score of five).

One entrepreneur that we guided through this activity came out with the following results:

Canvas #1

- Problem: 5
- Customers: 5
- UVP: 3
- Solution: 4
- Channels: 5
- Revenue Stream: 1
- Cost Structure: 2
- Break Even: 2
- Key Metrics: 5
- Unfair Advantage: 3

Total: 35

After some analysis, this first canvas came out with a score of 35/50. It seems like there are plenty of potential customers in this space and they have a major problem that they need solved (fives in both problem and customer boxes).

The Unique Value Proposition is OK, but the solution and marketing channels are strong. That means this person believes he or she can easily reach ideal customers and have a great offer for them.

The big concern with this canvas comes in when we get to discussing the money. It doesn't seem like there is a lot of revenue to be made (only rated a one), the costs are probably higher (only rated a two) and the breakeven is low (a two).

The key metrics are easy to track (five) and the unfair advantage is OK (three). So, this canvas ranked pretty well overall, but the biggest concern/opportunity to improve is in being able to sell this solution for a higher price/margin and reduce the cost to create it. Low margins mean that we will have to reach a lot more people and sell a lot more products to achieve our goals.

Canvas #2

- Problem: 4
- Customers: 3
- UVP: 3
- Solution: 4
- Channels: 2
- Revenue Stream: 3
- Cost Structure: 4
- Break Even: 2
- Key Metrics: 1
- Unfair Advantage: 3

Total: 29

This second canvas came out with a score of 29/50. It appears that there is a decent amount of customers (three) and the problem is pretty strong (four). The solution is pretty strong as well (four), while the UVP is OK (three). The channels to reach these customers though is not that great (two).

The revenue streams are OK (three) and the cost structure is pretty good (four), but for some reason the break-even point is not that great (two). To add on, the key metrics were rated poorly (1) and the unfair advantage is OK (Three).

Initially this seemed like a great canvas, with a strong customer base, problem, and solution. But there seems to be a challenge with getting to the right customers, indicated by the low score in both channels and key metrics. Also, for some reason, the break-even score is low, even though both the revenue streams and cost structure are pretty good. So this has potential for success if we could resolve the issues with being able to build a path to the customers.

Canvas #3

- Problem: 2
- Customers: 5
- UVP: 2
- Solution: 1

- Channels: 2
- Revenue Stream: 4
- Cost Structure: 2
- Break Even: 2
- Key Metrics: 4
- Unfair Advantage: 2

Total: 26

With this third canvas, the customer segment seems strong (five), but there are some concerns that the problem isn't big enough (two). It also doesn't seem like the UVP is very strong (two) and the solution isn't great (one).

The marketing channels to reach the customer are not great (two). The revenue streams are pretty good (four), but there seems to be higher costs (two) and not a great break-even point (two). They key metrics are pretty good (four), but there isn't a big unfair advantage (two).

This canvas looks like it could use some additional research with the customers. There is a strong base, but it most likely doesn't have the right problem identified. This doesn't allow the UVP and solution to be clearly defined. Additionally, with strong revenue streams, if we could improve the cost structure, this could work out well.

By going through and doing this simple analysis on each canvas, you should have a good idea of the strengths and weaknesses of each idea. You will typically want to proceed with the one that has the highest score, which would be the first canvas in this case, because it likely has the best chance to succeed.

With that said, if you can resolve a particular canvas's problems and raise a lower score to a higher one, then you may want to consider it as well. For example, Canvas #3 could do very well if you can identify a bigger pain point with the customer base.

While the key is to pick the strongest canvas, the decision isn't immediately set in stone. You can always come back and explore one of your other ideas if the first one doesn't seem to work out after initial testing.

Once you have one selected, you will then move on to the process of testing each of your assumptions and updating the canvas based on what you learned. This is a *critical* step. Everything that you wrote down on your Lean Canvas is an assumption. It is your opinion, likely based on your knowledge and past experiences, but it is still an opinion. It isn't until we go out and systematically test, reflect, learn, and update it that we know for sure if it can turn into a successful business that will work for you. (More on that ahead.)

Customers & Problems

The secret behind creating successful businesses rarely comes down to the actual product and service offered. The specific thing that a business sells is important, but often times too much emphasis is placed on it. This is where many unsuccessful businesses get it wrong. This is where we got it wrong. Several times. When Tom created the idea for the "30 Days to Launch" product, he fell in love with that product. Then we focused all of our energy on creating *that* singular product. Then it flopped.

What did we miss? What should you be focused on if you want to create a successful business? The answer is simple:

Your future customers.

In order to find long-lasting success, you must shift your focus from *product* development to *customer* development. You must become *obsessed* with the group of people who you want to work with. You must fall in love with serving them. You want to be inside their heads. You want to understand their thoughts, emotions, challenges, aspirations, fears, and objections. You want to understand how they behave and what they spend money on and how they decide to spend their money. You want to know more about them that anyone else who is also trying to serve them. You want to better understand their problems than they even understand them. The better you understand your customer, the more successful your business will be. Why? Because everything you say will speak to them on an intimate level, and they will be raising their hands to work with you. Those who don't know of you will be attracted to your messaging. Those who do will sout your name from the rooftops. You will know who they are. You will be able to pick them out of a crowd. You know how they think and what they need.

Here is an example that a customer of ours named Dan sent to us. He joined our Lifestyle Builders program and was going through one of the training courses. In this course, we introduced our Ideal Customer Avatar, Sam, and described him—who he was, how he viewed the world, and how he felt. It was a basic stick figure image with Sam, his spouse & their 2 kids. This customer sent us his edited version of the picture (a simple X through "Sam" and writing in his name instead) along with the corresponding message.

"I'm going through Find Your Freedom intro video and thought it fitting to change Sam to Dan... This is exactly me!"

This is the result that you want to get from your customers.

Now, there is a specific order that you used when you filled out your lean canvas. There is a reason that you didn't think about money until Steps 6 and 7 (revenue streams and cost structure). There is a reason that you didn't think about your product or service until Step 4 (solution). And there is a reason that Steps 1 and 2 were focused on your customers and their top problems, along with Step 5, which is where to find these customers.

So that is where we will begin.

Let's say that you want to go fishing. (We are not sure why you want to go finishing, but it does allow us to give you a really good business analogy, so let's roll with it). What's your first step? You don't know until you answer a few questions:

1. What kind of fish do you want to catch?
2. Where will you go finishing?
3. Are the type of fish that you want to catch in the location where I plan to go fishing?

You can start by answering either the first or the second question, but regardless of the order, both questions *must* be answered before you head out. Because you need to know if the type of fish that you want to catch is in the location where you intend to fish.

Let's spend some time on that first question, "what kind of fish do I want to catch?" There are lots of different types of fish out there. Different types live in different bodies of water and eat different bait. Not all fish are lured the same way, so you have to use specific strategies when trying to catch a particular type of fish. For example, to catch a trout, you typically need a lighter line and a jerk bait. To catch a bass on the other hand, you are better off using a shredded worm lure and a skip bait technic. (*Note: these are just two examples we threw out there, please consult a professional fisherman/fisherwoman for real-life advice!*)

You can't say that you want to catch every type of fish, because it won't help you narrow down where you should be fishing, what type of bait to use, and what strategy to use—therefore instead of catching every type of fish you catch no fish. If you ask a fisherman what type of fish they are trying to catch, they will tell you the specific type of fish, such as bass or trout. You will also then see that they picked where they want to fish based on the type of fish that they want to catch. They also picked their equipment, including their fishing pole, type and weight of fishing line, and bait, all based on the type of fish that they want to catch. They will also probably tell you that they are fishing at that specific time because that is when the fish are ready to bite.

The second question will help you know where you look. You can go fishing in just about any natural body of water; a stream, a river, a pond, a lake, a sea, or an ocean. If there is water, then you can fish. But if you are fishing in a place where the fish that you want to catch are not, you will not be very successful.

Much like starting a business, anyone can pick up a stick, put some string on it, dangle it in a puddle and say they are fishing. But only prepared fishermen know each type fish well enough to find success—and catch a load of fish. If the fish are not biting, the fisherman will start looking for the problem and a solution. Maybe there are no fish in this location, and they need to go to a different location. Maybe they are using the wrong bait and will try different bait, or maybe their strategy forecasting and reeling the fish in doesn't jive with how the fish wants to take the bait and they need to change it up.

Anyone can call themselves entrepreneurs because they come up with an idea, create a product, put it on a website and list it for sale. But unless they understand their customers inside and out, they are no different than the fisherman who picks up a stick and fishes in the puddle. It doesn't matter how hard they try, they won't achieve success because various pieces are not properly connected to allow that success.

So, to be a successful entrepreneur, you need to think like a fisherman.

- What kind of fish do I want to catch (people to serve)?
- Where will I go finishing (find those people)?
- Are the type of fish (people) that I want to catch in the location where I plan to go fishing?
- What type of bait should I use to catch these type of fish (offers)?
- When are the fish (people) biting?
- How do I get more fish (people) biting?
- What equipment do I need to catch these fish (people)?

What Kind of Fish Do You Want to Catch?

The first question to answer is "which type of fish do I want to catch?" or "what type of people do I want to help and have as my customers?"

These are your future customers, and the better you understand who they are, the more successful you will be as an entrepreneur. This step is often the one that most entrepreneurs spend the least amount of time with and end up causing themselves much more frustration and stress later on when no one seems to be buying.

If you've been in or around business for any length of time, you may have heard any or all of these phrases: customer persona, customer avatar, ideal customer, ideal customer avatar, etc. Even though each of these terms may have their own nuances in meaning, they all coalesce around the same idea of understanding your future customer. For the sake of simplicity, we will use Ideal Customer Avatar (ICA) to refer to them for the remainder of this book.

So, let's first define what we mean when we say ICA.

Ideal Customer Avatar (ICA) - A fictional person or character who helps you understand who the *perfect* person is to purchase from your business.

If you are targeting to help individual people, then this ICA will work just fine. (If instead you are targeting businesses, then you will want to create a profile for the type of business that you want to serve, as well as for the specific person within that business that you will help.) This doesn't mean that this will be the only person to purchase from your business, but it will help you make decisions based on specific needs of your ICA. Others, of course, will likely need the same of similar things, but this helps you stay focused.

Defining who your ICA can be a challenge, but the benefits from spending some time to create this are monumental. When you have clarity on who you do (and don't) want to work with, it will help make decisions easier and aid in problem solving when things aren't working.

There are two major areas to consider when you are defining your ICA. The first is what you are likely familiar with; their age, gender, marital status, income level, etc. These are known as *demographics* and have long been used in marketing. They are typically hard facts about a person. Demographics are a nice start to getting to know your ICA, but they often don't go deep enough to really help you understand what motivates them to buy. So you also want to identify things, such as; their values, beliefs, fears, etc. These are known as *psychographics*, and let you get a much deeper understanding of how people think and behave. When combined, these will help you get a complete picture of your ICA.

To simplify: Demographics help you define *who* your customer is, while psychographics help you understand *why* they buy.

Here are a handful of questions to ask:

Demographics:

- How old are they?
- Are they male or female?
- Where do they live?
- What is their occupation?
- How much money do they make a year?
- Are they single or married?
- Do they have children? How many?

Psychographics:

- What books or magazines do they read?
- Who do the idolize/follow?
- What are their hobbies?
- What do they enjoy buying?
- Where do they congregate?
- What are their aspirations?
- What are some of their core beliefs?
- What do they fear?

- What are their pain points/needs?
- What are their delight factors/wants?
- How do they think and feel when it comes to their pain points?

This can often be a challenge the first time you do it. You may feel like it takes too much time, but *do not skip this*. Learning the demographics and psychographics is the foundation of your business and putting in this work will save you lots of frustration, time and money in the long run and, most important, lead to more success.

Here are a few things to avoid when creating your ICA:

- **Multiple Avatars:** The point of creating an avatar is to be able to help you focus and make decisions. Some people will argue that they have multiple avatars, but you want to avoid this. Trying to target multiple types of people at once will make decisions more difficult and move your service or product from a specialist to a generalist, which you want to avoid.

- **Making Your Avatar Too Broad:** Another challenge some people have when doing this activity is that they make their avatar generic. They don't go deep enough, which doesn't give you real insights into how they think and act. You want your avatar to be unique, so don't be afraid to dig deep. Remember, just because you are defining your avatar doesn't mean that this is the only person who will buy. Instead, it means that this is the perfect person for your offer, but many other people with similar needs will buy as well.

- **Not Having a Pain:** Another objection that often comes up when creating an avatar is that the people you want to help or the offer you sell doesn't solve a pain, such as helping someone book a luxury vacation. Remember, people spend money to solve problems. Someone who wants to go on a luxury vacation has a need/want and there are ways to help them get what they desire.

- **Isn't This Just Made Up:** Some people struggle as to the value of this activity, saying that they have just guesses/made up the answers in their heads and this isn't a real person. Who knows, maybe none of this is right anyways? You are right. At this point it is made up, based on your experience and assumptions. Ultimately you will start validating/invalidation this avatar and make changes based on real people.

Where Should You Go Fishing?

Now that you know the fish you want to catch (the businesses or people that you want to serve), you now need to figure out where those people are. If you don't know where they are, you won't be able to catch them.

When you filled out your Lean Canvas, you should have initially defined this with the channels box. You expanded on this as you created your ICA and defined some of the psychographics, such as where they congregate and what hobbies/interests they have.

Here is a list of questions you can ask to expand on this:

- Do they congregate in a group of similar people somewhere?
- What kind of content (videos, audio, written text) do they consume?
- Is this group online (FB Groups or online forums) or a physical location (coffee shops, conferences, local meetups)?

For example, we know our avatar Sam the entrepreneur often seeks out other entrepreneur communities. He wants to find others who understand his struggles, a place he can ask questions and find out information. So our channels on our Lean Canvas would include Entrepreneur-focused Facebook Groups and live events (conferences and masterminds). We also have found that Sam likes to listen to podcasts.

When Are the Fish Biting?

With clarity on what type of fish you want to catch and where they are, the next thing to look at is when they are biting. Tom's grandfather used to make them get up super early when they would go out fishing. When Tom asked why this was, his grandfather's response was "that's when the fish are biting."

For someone to purchase your product or service, it has to be the right time for them. This typically involves a few things coming together to make it the right time:

- They need to be aware of the problem.
- They have to be aware of the solution.
- The pain they face or pleasure they receive has to outweigh the cost.

When someone has the above criteria checked, they are a "hot" lead. For example, let's say you are driving to an important meeting and you experience car trouble, preventing your car from moving. You are stuck on the side of the road.

You are now aware of the problem and need a solution. You pull up your phone and search for a company that can tow your vehicle. You were aware that a tow truck was a solution, and you found a company that offered that service. So, you have found a solution. If you don't get your vehicle towed and fixed, you won't be able to drive to work. It is totally worth it to pay the towing company to tow your car to a mechanic. So, you paid the towing company and they towed your car to the mechanic.

This process that you just went through was your *customer journey*. What does that mean?

Customer Journey - The process and experiences that a customer goes through before buying, while purchasing, and after becoming a customer.

In the tow truck example above, the customer journey was pretty short. You were ready to buy and didn't need much support or nurturing along the way. You were aware of the problem, it was important and urgent, you found a solution and you became a customer (although not necessarily of ours). This is not always the case. Sometimes customer journeys are longer and there is more of a need to nurture potential customers through the process. There are different ways to define your this, but we like to sum it up with the five below phases:

- **Awareness** - During this phase, the person becomes aware of the problem he or she has and potentially your company/solution.
- **Consideration** - During this phase, the person is researching, considering his or her options, and figuring out if he or she actually needs a solution, and which one may be best most ideal.
- **Conversion** - During this phase, the person makes a decision, purchases a solution, and becomes a customer.
- **Retention** - During this phase, the person has a great initial experience as a customer and ongoing experience as a customer, including being able to make additional purchases to continue solving the initial problem (if needed) and to solve new problems that arise.
- **Advocacy** - During this phase, the person has such a great experience as a customer that he or she tell and refer other people to your company.

Each customer will go through each of the first three phases. Some will have a more urgent need and progress through it quickly, as in the case of the tow truck above. Others will progress through at a slower pace and require more nurturing to help them become a customer. This is where most businesses stop. If you go above and beyond for the customers by focusing on retaining them and having them become advocates, you will not only build loyalty, but also allow your customers to become your best advocates and generate new customers for you.

Once you've defined your ICA, your next step is to map out what you believe the ICA's customer journey looks like. If your ICA is you in the past, which is common if you are solving a problem that you experienced and overcame, then think about how you went through this journey. If it isn't you, step into the shoes of your ICA and start thinking like he or she would think.

- How do you become aware of the problem and need? How do you become aware of the company/product?

- What education do you need before you make a purchase decision? Where do you go to find this education?

- What objections do you have that stop you from making a purchase? What needs to happen for this pain to be big enough and important enough to solve it now—and why would you purchase from your company as compared to a competitor? What needs to exist to make this purchase as simple as possible to complete?

- After you purchase, what happens next? Are you guided through the process? Do you get the product/service in a timely manner? Does it meet your expectations? What unexpected surprise would put this over the top for you? What would make you come back and purchase this product or from this company again?

- What would need to be true for you to have such a great experience that you want to share it with others? Is there an easy way to share it, and what benefit do you receive for sharing it?

By answering these questions, you will start to map out an initial journey for your customers, which will help you understand the process that they will likely go through. This allows you to design your business to support these people and help them solve their problems by becoming customers.

We learned a lot about our customer journey through the use of our free Facebook group at the time, Family Entrepreneur Life. We knew who we wanted to attract – "Sam" – and we created our messaging to match those psychographics. We used the group to get to know our members, and to get really clear on who those ideal clients were. It also allowed us a place to see what kinds of content our ICA asked for and consumed.

If at any point during this process you are not sure the answer to a question, go out and do some research. As part of filling out your Lean Canvas, you've identified where you believe these people congregate and how you can reach them. You've also listed existing alternatives, which are basically other things that people would turn to solve the problem today. Spend some time where they are and get to know them. You can learn a lot by reading what they read (books, magazines, blogs), listening to what they listen to (audiobooks, podcasts, music), watching what they watch (shows, movies, online videos) and seeing what they say (product reviews, group/forum posts). Additionally, when you find where these people congregate, you can even ask them some questions or have them complete a survey. All of these methods will allow you to better understand your customers, their pains, how they think, and what their journey looks like.

Talking to the Fish

At this point, you should have a pretty good picture of not only what your ideal customer looks like, where you can find them, and the path that you believe they will take to not only become customers, but to have a great experience with you.

That all sounds great, but how do we know if it is even right? As Steve Blank, author and adjunct professor of entrepreneurship at Stanford says, you must "get out of the building." Far too often we think that we have all of the answers. Instead, you are way better off to get the answers by talking to the fish (your ideal customers).

It's usually at this point when we tell people that they need to talk to their ideal customers that they get nervous and throw out excuses as to why they aren't ready to talk to people: "but I don't have a product yet" or "I don't know where to find them" or "I don't know what they look like" or "I'm afraid to talk to people." (Note: If you're afraid to talk to people, you're going to have a tough time starting any business—but we'll get to that in a moment.) So, let's take time to tackle each of those.

- **"But I don't have a product yet"**-Correct. You don't need a product to talk to people. In fact, it is better if you don't. Your goal of these conversations is to *deeply* understand your ICAs. These are conversations for you to ask questions, get to know them, and validate/invalidate what you initially identified as your ICA, their top problems, and where to find them. You can lead these conversations with "I am trying to help people with X problem or do Y better, do you have a few minutes to chat and share your experience with this?"

- **"I don't know where to find people"**-You had some initial ideas when you filled out your Lean Canvas (Step 5 - channels). Additionally, when you created your ICA, you identified some places that these people congregate, as well as some of their interests. Use that as a starting point. You can also spend time checking out the potential alternatives that you identified on your Lean Canvas, which is basically a list of your competitors. Even just starting to have conversations with a few people will help you identify more places to find others like them, including directly asking them who else they know whom you should talk to.

- **"I don't know what they look like"**-You should have an initial idea after filling out your ICA. Don't worry, this is not supposed to be perfect. It is through conversations that you gain more clarity on what your ICAs look like, as well as what they don't look like. People often don't realize it but identifying who isn't your ICA is often just as valuable as those who are.

- **"I'm afraid to talk to people"**-What makes you afraid to talk to people? Ask yourself that question and really explore it. You talk to people every day, right? These conversations are some of the easiest to have because you are basically asking questions. You are not positioning yourself as the expert, but instead positioning people that you are talking to as the experts. You are not selling them anything, but instead trying to better understand and help them solve their problem. Also remember, most people enjoy talking about themselves, especially when you express an interest in something that is on their mind.

It can feel a little uncomfortable to put yourself out there and talk to people, but we promise you, it gets easier with time. If you want to build a successful business, not only will you have to do things that are uncomfortable and challenge you, but you will have to be OK with it.

Now that we ruled out the excuses, how do you actually go about finding these people and what do you say to them?

Let's start with how to find them. Here are some great options:

- People You Know: Family, friends, acquaintances, people you only connect with once a year to with them a happy birthday on Facebook (you catch my drift). Start by making a list of people who you know that may be your ICA or at least interested in this topic.

- People with Interest: As you were doing initial research, you may come across people who have stated that they suffer from the problem you are trying to solve. For example, they may have posted in an online forum asking for help with a trout-catching problem. Make a list of these people and reach out. You also look for people who have expressed interest in your product. For example, if you asked a question or created a survey and shared, those who responded are prime people who may be willing to hold a quick conversation with you. You can also do a search online through various website for people who fit your ICA, or go to a physical location of where your ICA congregates and talk to people there—such as a specific store or industry conference.

Through the above two methods, you should be able to easily create a list of at least 10 people who are willing to chat with, but the more the merrier. Now it's time to reach out to this list of people. Pick whichever methods you've communicated with them in the past, or what seems like the most logical. This might be an actual conversation with someone if you see them in person, or it could be a text message, email, social media mention, etc. Typically, the more personal and direct form of communication, the better.

What do you say when you reach out? Something along the lines of this tends to work pretty well:

"Hey Jim.

Hope all is well. It's been a while, but I look forward to seeing you and the family at the annual picnic in a few weeks.

Anyway, I'm thinking about starting a new business to help

people manage the stress in their lives. As you know, I struggled with this for a long time and it lead to some pretty serious health issues, and I believe that there are a lot of people out there who face this challenge and could use some help.

I know you've mentioned this being a challenge as well in the past. Before I get too far along with this idea, I'd like to chat with a few people to make sure that it truly is a problem and it is worth pursuing. I don't have a product yet, so I don't have anything to sell you. I'm just at the information gathering stage. Would you be willing to chat for a few minutes on this? If so, I'm free Monday from 12-1 or Tuesday from 8-3.

If this isn't a good time, I understand. Do you know anyone else whom I should chat with on this topic? If so, would you be able to connect us?

Thanks, and I look forward to seeing you in a few weeks."

This is just an example, but let's analyze it.

- We addressed the person by his name.
- We personalized the message to him. This can be related to how we know him or how we found him, for example, if they posted something online.
- The middle of the email is a generic message that you can reuse, which explains our request, why it is important, and what you are looking for.
- The middle of the email also emphasizes that you won't be selling this person anything, as that is often a reason that people would choose not to respond.
- At the end, you invite him to have a conversation, and ask if there is anyone else whom you should speak with. Provide him with a few times that you are free, or provide with him a link to where they can schedule time with you.

This is just one of many examples. You can craft your own message to fit your style and language—just remember that the goal is to get a conversation with this person. Making these messages personal, complimenting something that the contact has done, or giving him or her something that of value are all powerful techniques that you can add into this initial message to increase the chances of having a conversation. Each of these messages will take a little bit of time to create, but your response rates will be much higher than just sending the same message to everyone. Also, early on in your business you want to focus on the quality of people and getting deeper to better understand them.

Once you get some conversations confirmed, you want to shift your focus over to planning out how these conversations will go. You have a few main objectives with these calls:

- **Ideal Customer Avatar Clarity:** Further understand and refine your ICA. Determine if this person would be a good client or not and update your ICA profile as you get more clarity.

- **Problem Clarity:** Focus on understanding your ICA's top challenges, including descriptions of the problems and how important solving them are to your ICA. Using the exact words and phrases that potential customers say can be powerful in your marketing.

- **Competition Clarity:** Understand how they have already tried to solve this problem. This will help you understand what else is out in the market and allow you to determine how to be different and position your solution in a way that matters.

- **Marketing Channel Clarity** - Understand if you are able to find your customers. You eventually want to be able to sell to these people, so you want to make sure that you know where you can find them and that there are enough of them.

There is no single way to handle customer interviews. There are many good approaches out there, but the most important thing is to have a basic script/process that works for you. In his books *Running Lean*, Ash Maurya recommends the following approach:

Here is a basic format that you can use for these calls:

- **Welcome (2 Minutes - Set the Stage)** - Briefly describe how the interview process will work.

- **Collect Demographic Info (2 Minutes - Test Customer Segments)** - Collect some basic demographic information to help you segment and qualify early adopters.

- **Tell a Story (2 Minutes - Set Problem Context)** - Share a brief story that explains why you are working on solving these problems and see if any of the problems resonate with the interviewee.

- **Problem Ranking (4 Minutes - Test Problem)** - State the top one-to-three problems and have the interviewee rank them. Inquire if there are any other top problems that they have that you didn't mention.
- **Explore Customer's Worldview (15 Minutes - Test Problem)** - Go through each problem and dive deeper. Ask the interviewee how he or she addresses them today. This also lets you understand more of their psychographics.
- **Wrapping Up (2 Minutes - The Hook & Ask)** - Wrap up with two questions. The first is if it is OK to reach back out if you proceed and come up with a solution. The second is if he or she could introduce you to other people with similar interests whom you should have a conversation with.
- **Document Results (5 Minutes)** - Take a few minutes and document the results while they are still fresh in your mind.

We used this approach for a while, then adapted it based on what personally worked for us. What we discovered was that as we started having these conversations, they became less structured and more natural. We still were able to collect important information while having more of a conversation. Whatever approach you use, the key is to ask questions but try not to lead the people you interview. You really want to be able to explore and understand things from their perspective so that you can learn and validate/invalidate/update your initial assumptions about who your ICA is, what your ICA's top problems are, how to find your ICA, and who your competitors are.

Continue having conversations with people until you get to the point where the responses become predictable. This might come from 20 conversations, 50 conversations, or more. Although you likely want to move ahead, don't rush this part. Continue talking to people until you get to that point of pretty consistent and predictable answers. Also realize that customer research never actually stops. You should always be having conversation with existing and potential customers to stay connected and understand their needs.

Additional tips for this:

- When trying to chat with someone, think about WIIFM (What's In It For Me)? Offer them something in exchange for taking the time to chat with you. Sometimes these discussions help the person we talk to increase their clarity. Other times we've offered to help them with a problem in exchange for the call. Another idea is to create something from the calls and share it out. For example, we ran a special series called "Couples and Entrepreneurship" on our podcast and a bunch of different entrepreneurial couples agreed to come on. We got to spend anywhere from 30-60 minutes with these people and ask them questions. This benefited them by gaining some needed exposure in front of our audience. Think of what you could offer people.

- Try to avoid taking notes while doing these interviews. When possible, see if you can record the interviews. If you are in person, you can use a recorder or your smartphone. If these are being done via phone or video calls, you can use a call recorder. This will allow you to focus on the interview and not get distracted trying to capture everything in real-time.

- Really focus on the pain they are experiencing and how they view it/ describe it. This is how they see it, and how you will describe it when you market to them in the future. Some people you talk with will not be aware of their problem, they just know they are in pain. Or they, not being the expert, may think they have one specific problem, but you know that it is actually a different issue altogether. This can often be described as them identifying a surface level problem, while you know the root cause. It can also be them describing the *what they want* vs. *you knowing what they need*. They are not wrong, this is how they see the problem, and how you want to explain it to them, so that you can ultimately help them see and fix the real problem. But initially, you need to talk to them about the problem they see *before* diving into the problem *you* see, or they won't value your solution.

- Also, be sure to focus on the ultimate benefit/transformation. What will their life look like once this pain has been removed? How will they feel? What will they then be able to do that they can't do now?

This process of understanding customers and their problems should never really end. Stay curious. Don't stop learning. Always continue talking to potential and existing customers. This will not only keep you connected to shifts and changing needs, but it will also be one of the strategies to continually bring new customers in. As you will see, going through this approach will actually result in a portion of these people that you talk to becoming your initial set of customers.

Solutions & MVPs

L et's check in on where we are at. At this point you should now have a pretty clear idea of your ideal customer, their top problems, how to find them, and some of the top competitors. Beyond what you initially filled out on your Lean Canvas, you've done some research and have actually talked to a bunch of your ideal customers. As a result, you now know and understand them much deeper. You understand not only the pain that they are experiencing, but also how they describe it, how they view the problem, and their concerns of what will happen if they don't find a solution. As a result of this, you should have found a group of people with a pain/problem that is real who need a solution with whom you want to work. If you haven't, do not proceed yet. Instead, either continue exploring this canvas to see if you need to shift your avatar, your problem, or your marketing channels. If that doesn't work, there may just not be enough with this Lean Canvas to warrant proceeding and trying to build a business around it, at which point you can go back to one of other ideas that you initially brainstormed and repeat the process.

In case you missed it when we said it above: If you don't have clarity on these areas yet (and a real problem that this group needs solved), be sure to schedule more customer interviews and talk to more people. Don't skip ahead without clarity or you will end up repeating what we did with our 30 Days to Launch program. You will spend a lot of time, money, and energy trying to build a business that just won't work.

If you *do* have clarity in these areas, you now get to move on to the typically more exciting aspects, which are coming up with (and confirming) your solution.

When you first created your Lean Canvas, you outlined your initial thoughts on what your solution would look like. This solution was based on who you thought your ideal customers were and the top problems they were facing. Now that you have held your customer interviews, you have made some updates to those sections of your Lean Canvas. Look at some of the other sections and see if they need updates as well.

The third box is your Unique Value Proposition (UVP); in other words, what makes your business different and worth paying attention to. After your research and talking to lots of potential customers, you will likely have a bigger list of competitors (existing alternatives) and gaps that they have in their products or services that are not solving your ideal customer's pain. These gaps expose themselves as the problems that the people you talked to still have, even after trying some of the initial alternatives. Update and hone in on your UVP as needed.

Next up is the solution box. Ideally you have a solution for each problem in the problem box. Again, these problems may have changed and definitely have been refined based on your conversations, so review your initial solutions and make any adjustments. If you uncovered new problems during your interviews, those will require new solutions.

You've likely already updated your (marketing) channels box. If not, make any adjustments that you need there, eliminating channels that didn't work and adding in ones that did. This learning will make it easier to find and sell your solution once you create it.

In addition to the previously mentioned boxes, we will also look to update and confirm the information related to the revenue streams, cost structure, and break-even boxes.

Your goal with this next phase is to shift the focus beyond just the customers and their problems and towards a solution and business model. At the end of this phase, you want to have a solution that your ideal customers are excited about, as well as confirmation on the financial numbers on your Lean Canvas. You need proof the plan is viable, meaning that customers will pay the price that you want to charge and that you can produce the solution low-cost enough to build in a good margin that will allow you to pay yourself what you desire, generate a profit, cover your taxes, and cover all of your business expenses.

What Kind of Bait Should You Use?

Going back to our fishing example: We have confirmed the type of fish that we want as well as the location of those fish. Now that we know where the fish live, we need to use the right bait to attract them. Bait selection is critical when fishing. If you select the wrong bait, you won't attract the type of fish that you want, and you will likely attract the type of fish that you don't want (or no fish at all). So, the key to selecting the right bait is to find what simultaneously attracts the fish that you want while repelling the fish that you don't want.

This is the same approach that you want to take with your ideal customers. You want to offer something that they will love and will attract them to you but repel people who are not ideal customers. If you select the wrong bait, you may begin attracting the wrong people who won't become customers. For example, if your bait is giving away an Amazon gift card, you will attract a lot of people. But if the problem that you want to help people solve is with helping them lose weight, you will attract a whole bunch of people who want a free gift card but who may not care about losing weight.

When thinking about your bait, you actually want to start with a principle that we discussed earlier in this book: start with the end in mind. Just like you needed to understand what you wanted your business to look like so you can build a path to achieve it, you need to understand what your ideal customer wants to achieve so that you can build a path to help them get there. What is the ultimate result that your ideal client wants to achieve by solving their problem? What will their life look like after the pain has been removed? How will they feel? What will they then be able to do and experience that they want but don't have now?

This is where you really start to benefit from the work that you've done thus far with your customer interviews. At this point, you should really start feeling clear about your ICA, specifically their psychographics, top pains, and desires. You've heard the words and phrases that they've used to describe their challenges and what result they want. This will give you what you need to create the perfect bait to attract them.

Typically, the bait that you use will be focused on solving their pain. It will first identify their pain, which they are currently experiencing, then show them the process for resolving that pain and invite them to get started. Imagine that you have a headache. You know your pain is that your heads hurts. When you seek to stop the pain, you will be attracted to something that is advertising to people with headaches and promises to stop the pain, such as a pain medication. The medication will temporarily stop the pain. It addresses the symptoms of the pain, but not the root cause. There could be many underlying reasons for someone having a headache, such as poor blood flow. The ultimate solution is to fix the blood flow issue, but someone with a headache may not know that that is the problem, so they wouldn't be attracted to something telling them that it can fix their blood flow. They are attracted to something that fixes their known pain, which is their headache. *This is why it is so important to understand how they view and describe their pain, not how you do.*

Once you attract them by describing their pain and offering a solution, they then take the medication and their pain is removed. But their headache may come back. They can continue taking the pain medication, or they may now realize that the pain medication isn't solving their problem, so they seek a new solution. This is where you can now help them to see that although the pain and problem was a headache, that problem is actually just a symptom of a deeper underlying problem, such as the blood flow issue. Now that they are aware of that, you can then present them with the solution to fix their blood flow problem, such as your proven eating and exercise program. So, in summary, the bait that you attract your ideal client with is describing the problem that they are currently experiencing and aware of.

When Are The Fish Biting?

Tom's grandfather used to make them get up early because that's "when the fish bite." They usually stopped fishing by late morning before it got too hot, because the fish wouldn't bite midday. But they would return to the late in the evening, when the fish were biting again.

Going back to your ideal customer, it's important to not only meet them where they are, but also when they are ready to "bite." We previously discussed the ideal customer that had a headache. We need to meet them where they are, which is with the pain of a headache and looking for a solution. But what if this same ideal client was already aware that there must be a deeper/different problem, because they have tried the pain medications but are still getting the headaches? Well, they are at a different part of their journey, and the bait that we used to attract people earlier in their journey – the cure to their symptom, headache pain - won't work for this person anymore.

So how do you attract them so that you can help them? You have bait specific for this person at this stage of their journey. For example, you may now target them with messaging (on your chosen channels) around the fact that they've taken pain medication, but they are still getting persistent headaches, which is the pain that they are feeling now. They may be aware, or your messaging make them aware. You could then move to educate them that it could be a more serious issue, which they can identify by doing a survey/test that you offer. With this approach, you are now meeting this ideal client where they are located and using the right bait (the test) to attract them so that you can then sell them the solution to solve their problem.

Hopefully you are now seeing the benefit and value of having all of those conversations. Once you understand your customer, their ideal transformation/ end result, and where they are at in their journey, you can then offer them the right bait and solution to help them solve their current problem and either move them closer to their goal or allow them to achieve it.

Getting the Fish to Bite

When you begin attracting the right fish, some will bite, but likely others may not bite right away. The ones that bite realize they are hungry, see the bait, and take it—then you reel them in.

For others, the bait got them interested, and they may continue hanging around, but they don't ultimately bite. This is so frustrating, especially when you can see them swimming around the bait. Just take it already! Some will even take nibbles as they swim around, clearly showing that they are interested, but they won't commit.

Although we may get frustrated, it's important to realize that the fish need some help moving from being attracted by the bait to ultimately biting. Maybe they already ate, so even though they like the bait, they are not hungry/as hungry as they were previously. Maybe they have taken bait like this before and learned they didn't like getting hooked. Or maybe the other fish told them to watch out for this specific bait. (Fish talk to each other, right?) There could be many reasons.

So, what does a fisherman do in this case? If you are a fisherman, you then use different maneuvers to entice them. If you understand why they are not biting, you can address that and help them move to bite, or you just test different approaches out until you find the one that works. On one cast of the bait into the water, you might drag it across the bottom. On the next, you might let it sink a little, then jerk it, let it sink, jerk it, etc. On another, you may retrieve it quick so that the fish see it but aren't sure what it is. You may change up the location that they cast. You may also swap out/change up the bait. Maybe the first bait got them interested, but the second bait moved them to bite. Often times once they go through a few maneuvers and one fish starts biting, then other fish will begin to bite.

So how does this relate to your customers? Some may come to you because they saw the bait and they are ready to buy now. These would be your *hot customers*. You put the bait out there, they were attracted, their pain was high, and they purchased the solution because they believe it will get them the result they seek.

In fact, almost as if the universe was trying to give us a sign, as we were writing this section, we just took a break and saw someone post this online:

> *"I'm a buyer. I like to pay money to solve problems. There is nothing worse than trying to nurture me, ask me how you can help me, or try to build rapport with small talk. I value my time more than money. The more of the former you waste the less of the latter you'll get from me."*

If this is your potential customer, do you think this is important to know? If this person is attracted to your bait, they are likely hungry and ready to purchase. So, give them the offer and let them purchase already! These are the customers that you want to focus on attracting, as they are ready to buy, will take the least amount of your time, and often lead to most of your revenue and success.

But you will not always have hot customers. Some may have been attracted to your bait, but they don't take the next step to purchase and become a customer. These are warm leads. What do you do in this case? You nurture. If you remember when we discussed the customer journey, the first stage was *awareness*, which is where the bait comes in. The third stage was *conversion*, where they become a customer. But there was a second stage in the middle-called *consideration*. In this stage, the potential customer (often called a lead at this point), is trying to determine if they need a solution and, if so, what solution they should choose. Just like the fish hanging around the bait but not biting, these leads hang around your offer but don't buy. Your job is to help nurture them through this process. They have questions that they need answered or objections that are standing in the way of buying. For example, their pain may not be high enough yet for them to invest in a solution. They may be overwhelmed with too much information or too many options to make a decision. They may not trust your company yet or know if your solution will get them the results. They may not trust themselves to use the product/service. They may have been burned by other similar products in the past that didn't get them results, or maybe they are not seeing enough reviews/social proof that your product works.

So how can you nurture? You understand each of these reasons for expressing interest but not buying (often called *objections*) and you develop a process to help them clarify and move past each objection. Just like when fishermen try different casting and retrieving strategies, you can guide them through the process by trying different maneuvers to help them decide. The last thing that you want is a customer who hangs around but never makes a decision. You job is to move them along the process and help them choose. Any decision is better than no decision. If that decision is to become a customer, fantastic. If that decision is that they don't want to become a customer, fantastic. Your goal is not to make everyone say yes and buy your product, but to filter people through the process and get the right people to say yes and the wrong people to say no. When someone is on the fence and can't make a decision, it doesn't help them solve their problem, and it doesn't help your business. Imagine if people entered a store and couldn't make a decision on whether or not they wanted to make a purchase. Eventually they would clog up the aisles, not allowing them to solve their problem and making it difficult for the store to see who was really interested and needed help. It is much better for people who won't buy to leave the store than to hang around in limbo.

Let's clarify a couple things here:

- **The benefit to having a lead say no.** Your product is not for everyone, and if you try to make it so you will fail. People telling you no will give you more space to focus on those who are saying yes, and those are the opinions that count! It also gives you the opportunity to ask why they said no, and if you know that person is your ICA it gives you valuable insight into what changes you may need to make on your customer journey.

- **Are all people who say "no" the *wrong* people?** No, not necessarily. They may not be the right people, right now. We have had quite a few people who have wanted to work with us, but it wasn't the right time for them and where they were at. Ultimately, our messaging was so strong that as soon as the timing *was* right, they came back and purchased immediately! If they had gone against better judgement earlier, or we had tried to force them into a sale, they would not have seen success with the product, and we would have failed in serving them.

So how can you put this together so that you get the right sequence, messaging, and solution confirmed? You guessed it, by talking to your potential customers. Remember all of those people whom you already talked to? The ones who had pains and problems and seemed like your ideal customers? The ones who you asked "if it would be OK to reach back out to them if you ended up creating a solution." Those are the people who will help you get this all mapped out and confirmed.

Before you begin reaching back out, you will want to further define what you believe your solution will be and the path that you will take leads on to become customers.

Your solution should consist of the following:

- A way to solve each of the top problems that your ideal customers identified
- Features of the solution
- Benefits of using the solution
- Results the person can expect by receiving the benefits
- A potential name for your offer/process/solution
- A unique value proposition that makes it different from existing solutions in a meaningful way to your potential customer
- A price that you plan to charge
- A cost of what it will require to create & deliver the solution
- Proof that this solution has worked/will work

Now let's break each of these down into a little more detail.

- **Approach to Solve Top Problems** - For the Number 1 problem (or the top few problems), you want your solution to have a way to solve each problem.

- **Features** - These are factual statements about the solution, such as *what's in it*, *how long it is*, etc. These are the details of what's included in the solution.

- **Benefits** - These are what the customer will get as a result of the features. These answer the question: *So what?* This is the value that the customer gets from the features.

- **Result** - These are a step beyond the benefits, and ultimately what the customer is after.

- **Name** - This is what you will call the solution. Most people place too much emphasis on this, especially early on. If you don't have a name yet, don't worry. Just keep it in the back of your mind as you go through this process.

- **Unique Value Proposition** - You want your product to be different than the existing solutions, ideally in a way that stands out and solves the gap that existing solutions currently have.

- **Price** - How much you plan to charge the customer for the solution. This should be high enough to allow you to make the proper profit margin and fit into a zone where your customers will purchase.

- **Cost** - How much it costs you to create and deliver the solution. This should take into consideration the cost of materials or people to create the solution, as well as the cost to deliver and offer customer support afterwards.

- **Proof** - This will help the customer understand that it works. Early on, this may be more focused on who you are and why you create good things/should be trusted, but as soon as possible you want to have actual results and case studies from the solution and customers.

Here is an example: You are targeting people who exercise, want a solution to recovering faster from their workouts, and who value time and ease.

- **Approach** - Pre-mixed recovery shake so it can travel with you (ease). Saved time versus trying to mix your own post-workout shake (time saver).

- **Features** - 26 grams of protein, only 100 calories, pre-mixed

- **Benefits** - Faster recovery, increase muscle growth

- **Results** - You can become stronger, look better, and feel more confident without the constant soreness of typical workouts
- **Name** - Mr. G's Max Pump & Recovery
- **Unique Value Proposition** - Don't waste your workout! Pre-mixed and packed with everything you need, Mr. G's Pump & Recovery helps you recover faster and build more muscle.
- **Price** - $3
- **Costs** - $1
- **Proof** - Customer Testimonial - "I've tried a lot of workout shakes. Mr. G's is by far the best. It tastes great and I clearly notice that I'm not as sore the next day, even with a grueling workout. This allows me to have the beach body I desire without the usual fatigue and recovery time."

See how powerful laying out these elements of your solution are? It makes it easy to explain and understand, and hits on the pain and desires of your ideal customer. Regardless of if your solutions come as a product or service, you should be able to map out the above for it.

Also, an important note at this point: You do *not* want to put time and money into actually creating your offer yet. Instead, you want to instead craft your solution and begin gauging interest in it. Far too many people spend their time and money creating the product before they validate demand for it. This can lead to wasted resources if people don't want it. That's why validation before creation is so important.

So instead of creating the product, you are going to first create the *concept* of the product and see how your ideal customer responds to it. You are going to show it to them, walk through a demo and sales process like you would if you were actually selling them the product, without having the product. If you are like most people, this is when you ask us, "How am I supposed to sell this solution if I haven't actually created it?" The answer is the same way that you would if you had actually created it. You see, the risk that exists at this point is that you have the wrong solution and people won't buy it. So, through this process, you want to confirm all of the different aspects of the solution, which we outlined above.

To do this, you can create stand-ins for the solution. If it is a physical product, have a designer create an image of what you envision the finished product looking like. If it is a service/program, create a graphic of your proven process that you can walk them through. If it is a book, create an outline of the book and write the first chapter.

With your solution concept established, you will now reach back out to the people that you previously talked to about their problems and present the solution that you came up with. You can also add in some new people who maybe haven't gone through the first interview yet. This will not only let you test the solution, but also to see if you've nailed your ideal customer and can spot them. As with your first conversation, you want to be curious with this conversation and focus on learning.

Just like the customer interview, there is no single way to handle the solution interview. Here, we will continue with what Maurya recommends in his book *Running Lean*. We've modified this slightly from what was originally presented in the book, as this was split into two interviews: A solution interview and an MVP interview. Through our experience and all of the entrepreneurs whom we've worked with, we've often found that it can be more beneficial to combine these interviews into one. *Running Lean* is primarily focused on software and technology, whereas we've used this approach across all different industries and solutions.

Here is a basic format that you can use for these calls:

- **Welcome (2 Minutes - Set the Stage)** - Briefly describe how the interview process will work.
- **Collect Demographic Info (2 Minutes - Test Customer Segments)** - If this is your first conversation, collect some basic demographic information to help you segment and qualify early adopters.
- **Tell a Story (2 Minutes - Set Problem Context)** - Share a brief story that illustrates the top problems that this solution is tackling.
- **Demo (15 Minutes - Test Solution)** - Go through each problem and show how the solution solves that problem. Ask what questions they have, what resonated most, what they could live without, and what else is missing.
- **Test Pricing (3 Minutes - Revenue Streams)** - Let the customer know the price that you plan to sell this at and gauge their reaction.
- **Wrapping Up (2 Minutes - The Hook & Ask)** - Wrap up with 2 questions. The first is to ask them if they would buy this solution today. If

yes, collect their payment information. If no, ask why not and get their objections. Then see if you can follow up with them in the future if you close the gaps with their objections. The second question is if they could introduce you to other people like them with whom you should have a conversation.

- **Document Results (5 Minutes)** - Take a few minutes and document the results while they are still fresh in your mind.

The most valuable part of this interview is that question, *Will you buy this today?* The goal, especially with your initial conversations, isn't necessarily to get a yes. Your goal is to figure out what the objections are to buying. If they say yes, let them know that the solution isn't ready yet, but you can collect their payment information and will get them on the list to be one of the first to get it when it becomes available. If they say no, which they likely will, asking why not will quickly get you to understand their objections. The solution may be missing something, or the pain isn't high enough, or they lack trust in themselves, in you, or in the product. Understanding these objections will allow you to improve the solution, as well as further clarify and understand not only your ideal customer, but also their journey.

As you get this feedback, you will want to continue refining your solution and adjusting your process and messaging. You want to continue talking to people until you start getting more people answering yes to the question of whether they will buy. As this happens, you will have an initial list of people who either have already paid you or are willing to pay you.

Additional Tips For This:

- Even if you feel uncomfortable, don't skip over asking the "will you buy" question. It is easy for someone to tell you that it is a good solution, but the real test comes when you ask them to purchase. Businesses have failed because they believed what their potential customers said without ever asking them to commit. They then went and built the solution and were upset when only a small portion of people who said that they would buy end up purchasing. When money becomes involved, the truth comes out. Otherwise it is very easy for people to day it is a good idea when they don't have skin in the game.

If this feels uncomfortable to you, know that it is uncomfortable for most people. Building a business requires you to start getting comfortable with being uncomfortable. Also remember that your goal, especially the first time that you ask this question, isn't to get them to say yes, but instead to get them to reveal their true objections so that you can improve the product.

- When people pay you before you have a solution created it's called pre-selling. It is perfectly legal and a great strategy to use your ideal customers to fund your business. People often believe that they need to put a lot of their own money in, get a loan from a bank, or get an investor to make their business a reality. Using this approach, you are actually using your customers to fund your deal. This approach is used by a lot of businesses across various industries. There are even crowdfunding companies—such as KickStarter—that have a platform for people to pre-sell their ideas to their customers.

What Equipment To Use?

Fishing, not unlike most other activities, can start out super simple and get increasingly complex as you dive in deeper. Even though stores have aisles and aisles of fishing gear, anyone can buy a few basics and start fishing the same day. You don't need and shouldn't even be concerned with most of the equipment when you first start out. In fact, buying the "best" equipment will often not only cost you a lot more, but it will also overcomplicate the process, and not have any meaningful advantages to you at this point. As you complete several fishing expeditions, narrow in the fish that you want to catch, determine the best spots to fish, along with the best bait and strategy, then you can begin expanding and upgrading your equipment.

This same logic applies to your business. When you are just starting, you want to keep things as simple as possible. This first relates to your solution. The key thing to realize is that you will not be creating a single version of your solution, but instead you will launch many different versions of your solution as customers begin using it and providing feedback to you. The first version of your solution will not look like your final version.

This is how modern businesses creates new solutions. In the past, they would spend years developing a solution and releasing a feature-rich solution, hoping for big sales. Over the last few decades, companies have released that shifting to a lean agile approach to developing their solutions is much more effective. Instead of trying to pack all of the features into version one of their solution, they instead release version one with minimal features that solve the problem, then listen to user feedback to re-prioritize the next set of the features that the users want. Some of these features may already be identified, while others may not come out until the solution is released and being used.

For example, the first iPhone had fewer features than the current version. Apple did their research and figured out what features would be included. They then released it to their early adopters, got feedback, and continued to improve it. With each release, they enhanced it and included more features, moving beyond just selling to their early adopters and expanding to a wider audience.

If the approach is good enough for Apple, the world's first trillion-dollar company[6], then it should be good enough for you.

Creating Your MVP Solution

You are now ready to actually put your solution together. As we just discussed, instead of adding all of the potential features that you could into your first release, you instead want to focus on initially creating a Minimum Viable Product (MVP).

Minimum Viable Product - A solution with just enough features to solve the top problem(s), satisfy early adopters, and get feedback on the solution.

Up until this point we've only talked about the solution with our ideal customers. While this has been very helpful in allowing us to learn, there is also a limit to the value of this approach. You will learn a lot more once people use your solution. So, as you shift into this phase of creating your solution, you want to focus on creating an MVP and getting it into the hands of your customers as soon as you can. This MVP will be the least amount required in order to solve the problem. (Note: It may feel incomplete to you, embarrass you, and you may not want to release it. These are all-natural feelings, but do not let them hold you back.)

If your initial solution involves making a new type of cookie, make a single type in small batches. Don't worry about making different types or scaling up your cookie production yet. Focus on getting a handful made of one type, getting them to your customers, and getting feedback. If you are offering a service, focus on the least amount that you can include in that service and start delivering it. If it is a training course, consider delivering the course live the first time that you do it and incorporating feedback from actual students into it as you go. If you look back on the history of any successful product or brand, you will see that it has been an evolution, and what it looks like current day is drastically different than what it looked like when it first launched. So, don't compare your first version with your competition's 10th version, or your own future 10th version.

The key here, just like with the product interviews and solution interviews, is to keep learning. You will not have the perfect solution yet. Your costs will be higher now because you have startup costs and you are still developing your initial foundation.

Here are the minimum things that most businesses need when they launch their first version of a solution:

- A way to describe their solution to the customer, which we did previously by defining features, benefits, etc.
- A way to create the first version of the solution
- A way to collect money from customers
- A way to deliver the solution to the customers
- A way to collect feedback as your customers use the product
- A way to continue identifying potential customers and warming them up

What each of these looks like will vary based on your business and solution. The key is not to overcomplicate this. With everything at this stage, you want to implement only the minimum required. For example, you may not need a website yet. If you do need a website, keep it simple with your bait and a way to capture and nurture potential customers.

Launching & Initial Sales

With the previous steps completed, you now have prepared and are ready for your launch/opening! This is an exciting time. You open the doors, either physically or metaphorically, and begin serving people. You've put in a lot of work to this point, so this may seem like the end, but it is really only the beginning! Everything up to this point was pre-work, which has allowed you to get here. The goal now is to confirm that the pre-work you have done thus far has lined up the various puzzle pieces (your lean canvas) and get your initial set of the sales/customers.

Your First Fishing Trip

With all of the prep work behind you, you are now ready to finally go fishing! You feel like you are prepared, since you have a lot more clarity on the types of fish that you want to catch, where they are located, what bait will likely attract them, some strategies for reeling them in, and what equipment to use. Time to head out and start fishing!

But before you go, just a word of caution: This is where the bait meets the water. You've planned everything out and it seems like it should work but realize that things rarely go according to plan. Knowing that upfront is important. You may not catch any fish on your first fishing trip. You may have missed something in your prep work, or maybe it was just a bad day. Regardless of how many fish you catch, the key is that you got out there and began to fish. This is just your first of many fishing trips. After you complete it, you will be able to reflect on the trip and determine what adjustments you need to make next time to catch even more fish.

The good news is that all of the prep work that you put in will make your launch easier and more successful than if you hadn't. You're reaching out not to just any fish, but the types of fish that you want to catch. In time, and with adjustments from what you learn, your sales should pick up and continue to grow.

The Launch

Launching your solution to the world can be exciting, but also nerve-wrecking. A launch is an opportunity to generate buzz for your new product, so you must plan and coordinate accordingly. With that said, and this may be counter-intuitive, you actually want to keep your initial launch pretty small. Here's why:

- It's less work. Your goal with a launch is to get a group of people to purchase and then deliver a great experience to them. This is much easier to do on a smaller scale.
- It keeps your stress level down. Less things to worry about is important, especially the first time you do it. On subsequent launches/releases, you can build off what you did for this first one.
- It helps provide a great experience for your early adopters. You want this first set of customers to love the solution so that they get results and you can get case studies/testimonials. These help with marketing and selling in the future.
- It allows you to get feedback and improve. If you have too many customers, you will be overwhelmed and won't be able to listen and learn from your early adopters. Your business is not yet set up with systems and processes to allow you to handle a larger volume of customers. Focus on getting those initial customers, delivering a great experience, and learning.

Launches are typically broken down into three phases:

- Pre-Launch
- Launch
- Post-Launch

Pre-Launch

You have been participating in the pre-launch since you've started, which is all about getting ready to launch. You've been stocking your pond with leads. Now you want to plan out your launch, so you have to ask yourself some important questions:

- When will your launch be?
- How long will it be?
- Who will you be targeting?
- What special promotions/bonuses can you offer?
- What scarcity can you build it?

Most of the success of your launch comes down to how well you execute your pre-launch. If you've done all of the prior steps, you have now built a group of ideal customers, received clarity on their top pains/problems that they are willing to pay to have resolved, create a solution that solves their problems, and maybe even have a few people who have paid.

Whenever you go into a launch, you want to consider your objective. It's often useful to ask yourself, *what would make me feel like this launch was a success?* This would be your goal (or lagging metrics as we discussed earlier when talking about your personal goals). What you then want to do is think backward to what needs to come before to help you achieve that.

For example, let's say that you goal was to get 10 total customers. You already have two from your previous conversations. So, your goal would be:

Go from two to 10 customers by the end of the launch.

How you going to make that happen? What indicators/criteria can you assume to guide you?

Let's assume that with everything you are doing with your launch, you will convert 25% of your warm leads into customers. That means eight total customers divided by 25% conversion rate of warm leads means that you need a list of at least 32 warm leads. If you have fewer leads than this, you must have more conversations and get more leads before you launch. As you can see, the more leads you have, the more likely you are to achieve your target number of sales. If your conversion rate is 10%, then you would need 80 leads. The more work you do to get these leads before you launch, the more successful your launch will likely be.

You also want to design the onboarding and fulfillment process, which means what happens right after people purchase and become customers. What steps do they go through to not only get the solution, but to have a great experience and provide you with feedback. For example, when someone signs up for our business coaching program, they are welcomed into the program, given the ability to create an account to our training portal, and instructed to watch some initial training videos to get acclimated to how the program operates. This helps gives them a positive first experience, explains how to use the service that they just purchased, and sets expectations to help the get the most out of the service.

Launch

When you launch, you are now officially opening up for purchases. The key during a successful launch is to leverage the excitement and warm leads that you've created. Not only should you be advertising and marketing it, but you also want to continue to reach back out to each person you previously had a conversation with and work on getting them to purchase on day one.

Post-Launch

Once your launch is completed, things are just beginning. You want to not only make sure that each person who purchased had a great experience, but you also want to take some time to reflect and learn from it. Whether you make one sale or 100 sales, you are now open for business. The better you've clarified and tied the pieces of your business model together, the more likely your launch is to be a success. If you are disappointed with the initial results, don't fret too much. You had a certain level of knowledge before the launch. By taking action, you've now acquired new knowledge. How many total sales did you make? How many leads did you have going in? What was your actual conversion rate of leads to sales, and how did that compare to what you initially thought?

Reflecting on these questions will help you understand what pieces went well, what pieces didn't go well, and what changes you can make to close the gaps going forward.

Chapter 3.8

Growing Your Sales

With your launch complete, what is your next step? Where should the majority of your time, money, focus, and energy go in order to grow your business?

Restocking Your Pond

When you have spent the time to stock your pond, you can enjoy fishing for quite some time. If you continue to catch fish and take them out of your pond without restocking, you will eventually begin to catch less fish, and eventually might not catch any new fish.

The same concept goes for your business. You spent time throughout this process of finding ideal clients, warming them up, and putting them in your pond. You then went fishing and caught some of these prospects, turning them into customers and moving them from your "prospect pond" to your "customer pond." The cool thing about this is that you can then go fishing in both ponds, meaning that you can continue to fish in your prospect pond, converting prospects into customers. You can also then fish in your customer pond, turning existing customers into returning customers. Once they've purchased and have a great experience, they are more likely to purchase again.

The problem businesses face after a launch is that if they stop restocking their prospect pond, they'll slowly catch fewer fish. Without constantly finding new ideal clients, offering them the bait, and bringing them into your lead pond, your sales will stall.

This is where you will want to continue to focus on both the channels and metric boxes of your Lean Canvas. Your channels are where your ideal customers are and how you can find them. Your metrics will then help you track this customer acquisition process.

For example, let's say you have found a place where your ideal client congregates. You dangle your bait and your ideal customers are attracted. These leads then become aware of their problem and your solution, becoming prospects. You then move these prospects over your prospects pond and continue to nurture them. When they are ready, they purchase and convert them from prospects and into a customer, at which point you move them over to your customer pond, deliver the solution and continue to support and retain them. You do such a good job with this that they tell their friends about your solution, which then takes their friends from leads to prospects and restocks your prospect pond.

This is the entire lifecycle of your customer journey, which when done right will provide the means of restocking your prospect pond through existing customers referring others to you. Whether you use organic marketing (referrals, social media marketing, email marketing, search engine optimization, etc.) or paid marketing (pay-per-click, social media advertising, traditional media advertising, influencer marketing, etc.), it's important to establish at least one (and ideally multiple) strategies to restock your prospect pond.

Lifestyle Builder Starter Pack Resource
These Worksheets and Guided Activities will help you fill out your Lean Canvases and work through this section. This is included with your starter pack that you get for free with this book.
Get your free copy at www.lifestylebuildersbook.com

Section 4:
Setup & Scale Your Systems

Section Summary:

With your business model increasingly becoming more validated, starting with your initial set of sales and continuing with each subsequent sale, you will now shift into designing and organizing your business so that it can continue to grow and drive closer and closer to your goals. This section will walk you through the various areas of running a business and guide you through how to structure and organize for effective and efficient growth that doesn't take over your life.

Entrepreneurs Don't Get Vacations

Ariana's Take:

If you know us outside of this book at all, you probably have heard us referred to once or twice as the "Systems and Processes" people. That's thanks to Tom's background in consulting and project management and helping teams within corporations use Lean and Agile concepts to increase efficiency and workflow. (Woah, can you tell I've been hanging around with Tom for many years now? Sometimes it's like his words are coming out of my mouth!)

But it wasn't always this way. We didn't always have systems. And that often caused us big hairy headaches in our businesses, and, more importantly, our lives.

For example, take our real estate business: When we first started, Tom and his father were doing all the work on every property. There was no system to how they found, bought and renovated a property, which meant they usually ended up spending more than planned, so they saved costs by doing the work themselves.

What this meant for Tom, though, was that he spent nearly *every weekend* driving 45 minutes each way from our home to the properties in his hometown, working long and hard days installing drywall, running new plumbing/electric lines, tearing down roofs, painting (so much painting), and mudding and sanding all that drywall (he really hates drywall now).

For me, this meant lots of weekends alone, and having to explain over and over (and over again) to our friends, my family, and sometimes his own family, why Tom once again couldn't make it to that particular birthday, holiday, anniversary party or picnic. They couldn't wrap their heads around it, and I could tell even when they said they understood, they really didn't.

With no systems in place, the real estate business became a drain on our time, our money and our energy. In addition to Tom being gone on weekends, it always seemed like problems popped up unexpectedly at the worst times, stressing us both out. A tenant would call because their toilet wasn't flushing. Another could call because their power was off. Our insurance agent would inform us that our insurance was going to be cancelled in 48 hours because we missed paying a bill. It's like we were on call 24/7, not knowing what would come up, and trying to come up with a solution on the spot.

Now, thankfully, we had learned a bit when we opened the wine and liquor store. Like the importance of having processes in the office, an organization system for paperwork, and of handling our business finances. But this venture brought a new blessing and a curse to our systems—employees.

Again, our store is about 45 minutes away from where we live (apparently, we don't like to open our businesses close by…) but we set up a security system we could log into from home and used a printer/scanner in conjunction with cloud storage to keep track of all documentation we'd need. Simple!

Except for 2 things:

1. We opened with an employee hired, but she couldn't start until a week in.

This meant Tom and I worked the whole first week at our store! I took day shifts and brought the baby with me (9 months old at the time), and then Tom would drive down after work and take the night shifts. It was a system, but it sucked! We eventually hired in more part-time employees, but Tom would often have to drive down and take random weekend shifts that first year.

2. None of our employees were trained to handle inventory.

I continued to drive down once a week for an entire *year* to enter the new orders into our point-of-sale system. Every week, I spent hours figuring out what to order, only basing it off of imperfect reports from our point-of-sale system. I lost an hour and a half (86.4 miles round trip) of time to driving each of those days, with a young child in the back to entertain, just to return home to put the numbers in the computer and take care of any other pressing matters.

These are just a few examples of how not having a system at our store backfired on us. There are more—many more. Now I'm going to hand things over to Tom to tell you stories about how our systems evolved and actually *saved* our businesses, and made our lives a hell of a lot easier.

Tom's Take:

The first several years of our real estate business and our wine and liquor store, we didn't have businesses—we had jobs. Not only jobs, but jobs that demanded more, paid less, and caused us more stress than our regular jobs. There were many times when I (and eventually we) discussed whether we should just throw in the towel and get rid of them. Thankfully, we would discuss, and realize that the businesses were the key to living the future lives that we wanted. The problem was that we were not leading them very well. We had created additional jobs and had to move from doing all of the work into being the designer of a well-oiled machine that could operate without us being involved and doing every step.

Whenever we meet stressed-out and burned-out business owners, they all have similar feelings. They want to close down the business or sell it. The reason is because it is taking too much of their time, not making them enough money, and they can't step away. They can close it down, which means not generating any additional money, as well as losing what time, money and energy they've invested into it. They likely can't sell it, because they don't have a business. They have a job, and they are the employee and the business. To sell the business without them (the main employee) typically doesn't happen. People don't want to pay to acquire your headache, unless the business is making a lot of money and they know how to solve the problems that you are facing.

The solution to this problem is to intentionally design your business so that it is saleable. That is, set your business up so that it is not dependent on you. The funny thing is, when business owners do this, they typically no longer talk about closing down or selling the business. Why would they? They've created a business system that runs, provides them profit and a salary, and provides them the flexibility to live their lives the way they want. This is what we all desire, but often entrepreneurs are not intentional about designing their business in this way. Instead, they dive right in and just hustle to try and make it work. The problem is, you can only hustle so much before you can't hustle anymore. You need to work smart.

It took us a while, but we learned our lessons. As Ariana mentioned, there were several years where I missed get-togethers and important events because the businesses demanded our time. Luckily, I realized that I didn't want to continue this way and we began being a lot more intentional about implementing better systems to run our businesses.

In our real estate business, I began putting systems and processes in place. Each time we ran into an issue, I would not only fix the issue, but also create or update a process for how to prevent this issue and handle it in the future if it occurred again. I also began to make a list of everything we did and started targeting pieces to delegate. Each time we would buy a property, the purchase process was cleaner, and we started delegating more and more of the renovation work. This required less of my physical time, meaning not as many weekends away from Ariana and our kids.

When we opened the wine and liquor store, not only was I still working a full-time job, but I was finishing up graduate school as well. Given that the store was going to be open seven days a week, I couldn't physically be at the store most days and didn't want Ariana to have to be there. So, we thought about what the store systems needed to look like at the beginning. We created systems for how the store would run, defined roles and began hiring. We got creative and asked how we could do as much as we could without physically being at the store. Between hiring employees and implementing technology, we were able to mostly accomplish this. As time went on, we continued to hire and delegate (scheduling, inputting payroll, ordering inventory). This allowed us to get to a point where we physically only visit our store once every 90 days for a quarterly meeting with our main employees. Outside of that, we only spend a few hours every month dedicated to this business, which is mostly strategic planning, reviewing our dashboard and checking in/supporting our teams as needed.

Things look very different for us today. Rarely do I miss a family gathering. In fact, we've been able to take family trips for several weeks at a time, and the businesses keep on running. On our last family trip, a two-week vacation across the country, we only had one item come up that needed our attention. A hot-water heater broke, causing one of the basements of our property to get flooded. We got a message, coordinated an effort to resolve it, and 15 minutes later were back to our vacation. Additionally, we then put a process in place so that next time, we wouldn't have to be involved in the coordination at all.

We now have a third business, which is focused on helping entrepreneurs build the businesses that they need to create the lives that they desire (hence why we wrote this book). Whereas most people hear that we have multiple businesses and think we are crazy, what they don't see is that we are no longer creating jobs for ourselves when we start a new business or create a new offer, but instead are building businesses and systems that work for us and allow us to live the lives that we want. We want you to do the same, so this section of the book will show you how to design your business to support your ideal lifestyle and set up systems to continuously allow you to remove yourself from working in the business. This will not only contribute to your financial freedom, but also to your time freedom.

The Business Engine

Y ou've probably heard that an entrepreneur wears many hats. This is true. When you start a business, at least initially, you are likely doing everything in the business. Look at what you've been doing thus far.

- You've been doing marketing research and customer development as you identified your ICA and began surveying/having conversations with them.
- You've been doing product development when you created your solution.
- You've been doing selling when you converted people from leads into customers.
- You've been doing fulfillment when you delivered the solution to the customer after they purchased.
- You've been doing finance when you collected their money and began paying yourself, putting money aside for taxes, and paying your bills.

These are just a few of the many different things that you've been doing thus far. It you are not overwhelmed yet, you will be as you continue to grow your business. You will spend more time in each of those areas as you bring in more customers and will eventually reach a point where you are working all the time and not able to grow your business anymore. Most entrepreneurs eventually hit this point—it's called burnout (the physical and/or mental collapse caused by overwork or stress).

But wait. You didn't start your business to run towards burnout, did you? No. You started it to achieve freedom and the items that you listed on your life planner. So how do we rectify this so that you can achieve your goals and avoid burnout?

Answer: you build your business engine.

Engines are what keep a vehicle running, and they are what keep your business running as well. As your business grows, you want to keep improving and upgrading your business engine.

An engine in your vehicle is composed of several pieces; an engine block, flywheel, crankshaft, carburetor, etc. When combined and fueled with gas, your vehicle engine runs. Your business engine is also composed of four main pieces: marketing, sales, operation and finance. When these pieces are combined and fueled with leads and prospects, your business engine runs.

Let's dive deeper into these four pieces of your business. Your fuel is leads, which are ideal customers who may not even be aware of their pain/problems (or the fact that you exist). When we feed this fuel into your business engine, here is what happens.

- Marketing - Turns leads into prospects
- Sales - Turns prospects into customers
- Operations – Create and delivers solutions to customers and keeps them happy
- Finance - Collects money in and disburses it to where it needs to go

Right now, your business engine may be several individual components that have not yet been combined into an engine. You may be the engine tying these pieces together. While this worked to get you started, your engine will not function very well if you have to be in the middle of the engine and pulling all of the pieces together.

So, your goal here is to build an initial engine that can run on its own as long as you provide it with fuel (leads). Your first engine will not be a Ferrari engine. No, it will more likely look like a go-kart engine. At this point, you just want to build an engine that runs. As time goes on, you will work on upgrading your engine's various pieces to create a more powerful motor to support a growing business.

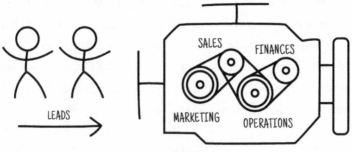

Your Business Engine.

Components and Processes

For each one component of your engine, you want to have a high-level process defined for how that component works and what part it plays in making the engine work. Once the process is defined, you will then you will want to use it—while continuously refining and improving it. Below are the six steps that you will follow to create and improve each component of your business engine.

1. **Create** - During the create step, you will define your process for the component, starting with the inputs and what initiates the process, the steps involved and when the process is finished.

2. **Analyze** - With the process created, you will implement it and identify issue areas/constraints. These areas are where problems occur or where things get stuck.

3. **Eliminate** - With the main problems resolved and the process working effectively (producing the right result), the next step is to eliminate waste and make the process more efficient, meaning we get the same result with less resources (time, money, and energy) consumed.

4. **Consolidate** - With extra steps removed, you will now look for areas where you can consolidate steps, which may include changing the timing or order of steps. What you are looking for here is the ability to, as the old saying goes, kill two birds with one stone.

5. **Automate** - With steps consolidated, you should now have an efficient process. Continue to take initiatives to streamline it with tools and technology.

6. **Delegate** - Finally, once you have the right tools and technology applied to the process, delegate any remaining work that you have to someone else.

The end result of this process is that you have a component of your engine that is working effectively (producing the right result) as well as efficiently (minimizing waste and maximizing resources). Additionally, some pieces of it are automated with the use of technology. The remaining pieces are being done by someone else so that your time can be focused on areas where you bring the most value. This is how you continue to grow without increasing the time that you dedicate to your business.

The below image is a quick sketch of what we use whenever we begin creating a new process.

PROCESS TEMPLATE

TRIGGER	MAJOR STEPS			END
‎	1	2	3	‎

SUBSTEPS	☐ — ☐ — ☐ —	POST
‎	☐ — ☐ — ☐ —	‎
‎	☐ — ☐ — ☐ —	‎

You can get a complete & fillable copy of this template
in the Lifestyle Builders Starter Pack at www.lifestylebuildersbook.com.

The goal for this section is to get your core processes created (Step 1 above). That is, each major piece of your business engine (marketing, sales, operations, and finance) should have a high-level process created. As you begin implementing these processes in your business, you will continuously go through the process of analyzing, eliminating, consolidating, automating, and delegating (Steps 2 to 6).

To create each of your core processes (and any other processes that you subsequently create), go through the following steps.

- **Process Logistics** - Define the name of the process, add a brief description, note the department (engine component) that the process relates to, name the owner of the process (who is responsible), and show the estimated time required and frequency that the process occurs.
- **Define High Level Process** - Each process consists of a trigger (what starts the process), 3-5 major steps, and an end (what signals that the process is complete). For each process, you will define these basic components at the highest level. For each major step, you can track a metric around the step to see how people are progressing through your engine components and the steps within each of them.
- **Define Detailed Process** - Each part of the process that you defined above can be broken down into smaller pieces. For the process trigger,

you will define what inputs/information is needed. For each major step, you will break them down into smaller steps. For the end, you will define any close out or post action steps.

The remainder of this section will be walking through each major aspect of your business engine and helping you to create your initial process. So, with that, let's dive into each of the four main pieces of your business engine.

Marketing

If you think of your business engine as a sequential flow that supports your customer journey, the first step in that flow is marketing.

When you created, and subsequently updated your Lean Canvas, you refined who your ideal customer was, their pains/problems, and where to find them. Throughout your research and interviews, you collected the words and phrases that they mentioned. We will now use all of this information to build the marketing pieces of your business.

The purpose of marketing is to attract ideal customers and nurture them through the process to be ready to purchase. Your marketing efforts will involve the first two phases of the customer journey: awareness and consideration. When you identify the different channels that you can use to reach your customers and dangle your bait in front of them, you will begin to pull them from *their* ocean and place them in *your* pond so that you can nurture them. It typically looks like this:

Generic Marketing Process

- **Trigger:** Bait is dangled in each relevant marketing channel
- **Major Steps:** Person takes the bait, becomes a lead, is nurtured, shows signs of being ready to purchase
- **End:** Lead is warmed up and ready to purchase

When the person takes the first step, which in this case is taking the bait, then he or she becomes a lead. Essentially, the lead is raising his or her hand and indicating interest. This may be confirmed by giving you an email address, calling a phone number, visiting your website or store, or whatever call to action (CTA) you had for them based on the bait.

It's important to point out that oftentimes marketing and sales will be combined into one component because it can be difficult to determine where marketing ends, and sales begins. The reality is that you're incorporating aspects of sales into the entire marketing process. The reason that we differentiate them is that at some point you need to convert your leads into prospects into customers. By separating these out, it is easier to focus on nurturing leads into prospects when we discuss marketing and converting prospects into customers when we discuss sales.

Sales

With your leads now nurtured through the marketing process and warmed up, the next component of your business engine is sales.

The purpose of sales is to convert your prospects into customers by having them make a purchase. As you continue to nurture leads through the process, you should begin to identify signs when leads are ready to shift to prospects. When those signs begin to show, you want to invite them into your sales process to further guide them to become a customer. Traditionally, it looks like this:

Generic Sales Process

- **Trigger:** Leads reach a point where they show signs of being ready to purchase
- **Major Steps:** Qualify leads, demonstrate solution solves problems, overcome objections, support decision making
- **End:** The prospect has become a customer by making a purchase

When it comes to sales, people often get afraid to ask for the sale because they fear that the prospect will say no. The goal of the sales process is not to get every prospect to say yes, but instead to guide them to make a decision. Some people will say yes, some will say—that's OK. The key is you don't want them to hang out in limbo without making a decision. That doesn't help them solve their problem if they can't make a decision, and it doesn't help you having a bunch of prospects whom you are not sure if they will purchase (thus wasting valuable time you could be spending on those who *will* purchase.

If they are not a right fit—not the ideal customer, it's not the right time, or another reason—it's OK to say no or have them say no. If they are a right fit, then you want to guide them to realize that and become a customer. It's important to realize that this basic process should be followed whether you are actually talking to the customer to make the sale, or if a website or other method is used. Essentially your marketing and sales process should support the customer on the first three steps of their journey.

Operations

If a prospect makes it through the sales process and decides to make a purchase, they become a customer. At this point, the focus is on creating and delivering the solution to the customer and providing them with a great experience.

Operations can be broken into two major pieces: solution creation/innovation and solution delivery/fulfillment.

Solution creation/innovation is the process for initially creating your solution (which you already have done) as well as improving and innovating on it based on feedback and customer need. Solutions rarely stay the same, therefore it is important to stay connected to your customers and the market to evolve your existing solutions and potentially create new ones. Here's a quick idea of how it looks:

Generic Solution Creation/Innovation Process

- **Trigger:** There appears to be an unmet demand/opportunity that is aligned with your business goals
- **Major Steps:** Fill out lean canvas, conduct problem interviews, conduct solution interviews, create MVP or add new features, launch product
- **End:** New solution or enhancements launched to customers

Once prospects purchase and become customers, it is important to fulfill the customers' order and provide them with a great experience. This delivery process really begins during the sales process with expectation setting and qualifying, but once they become a customer, your job now shifts to providing them with the solution and making sure that they have a great experience. Again, let's see what this looks like:

Generic Solution Delivery Process

- **Trigger:** Prospect makes a purchase, turning them into a customer
- **Major Steps:** Onboard customer, deliver solution, provide customer support, request feedback/testimonial, offer next logical purchase, provide easy way to refer others
- **End:** Customer has received his or her solution and is happy

Operations really cover the last two steps of the customer journey, which are retention and advocacy. You will retain them as customers by delivering a great solution and experience so that not only do they not ask for a refund, but they also become a repeat customer. It is much easier to sell to an existing customer than to a new one. Additionally, if they have a great experience, you can encourage and support them in sharing their experience with others. This will lead to your customers helping you with sales and marketing by sharing their experience and bringing you new leads.

Finance

You've probably heard the term "cash is king." Having cash is the key to staying in business. Therefore, your finance department is responsible for making sure that you collect the cash that is owed to you, manages and distributes the money to the various places that it needs to go, accounts for the inflows and outflows of money, produces financial reports to shows the health of the business and helps to plan for the financial future. Here's a quick walk-through:

Generic Solution Delivery Process

- **Trigger:** A sale is made
- **Major Steps:** Money is collected, money is distributed, books are updated, financial reports produced, budgets/forecasts are set
- **End:** Money is collected and accounted for

This is often one of the areas that intimidates people looking to start a business. Having a great accountant can assist you a lot and will be one of your best investments into your business. It will probably also be one of your first hires in the business. You will not hire him or her as an employee, but you will pay for the account's services and consider him or her a key member of your team.

This is also where we recommend that you implement Profit First. We first introduced this cash flow management system back in the Find Your Freedom section of this book to help you determine how big of a business you needed to meet your personal goals. While this system won't cover all of the financial needs of your business, it will help you with collecting and distributing money, along with supporting budgets and forecasts.

Chapter 4.3

Putting the Engine in Your Car

U p to this point you've been working on putting your business engine together. You've initially defined your high-level processes for each of the main components of your engine; marketing, sales, operations and finance. When these various components work together, they turn prospects into customers.

An engine alone though is not enough to get you to your destination. In Section 1 (Plan With Purpose), you laid out your personal goals and a roadmap to get there. In Section 2 (Find Your Freedom), we started to model what size business you needed in order to get you to your personal goals. Now you will take the engine that you built and place it into your business vehicle to drive you towards your goals. Just like a car has various systems besides the engine, your business will need additional pieces that will work in conjunction with the engine.

In addition to the engine, a vehicle is made up of various systems, including the driving and suspension systems, the electrical, exhaust, drivetrain, etc. Your business vehicle also has various additional pieces that are used in conjunction with your business engine, including leadership, people, strategy, dashboard, and cadence. When combined, these systems help focus and leverage the work done by the engine to get to the destination.

Let's dive deeper into these five additional pieces of your business. Your engine is what runs your business. When we place your business engine into a vehicle, here's what happens:

- Leadership - You set the vision and mission, and then lead your team
- People - You build a great team to support you in achieving the mission

- Strategy - The plan and decision framework to achieve the vision/success
- Dashboard - The view into the health of your business
- Cadence - The check-in process that you use to make adjustments

When your engine is dropped into a vehicle that also has these components, they can work together to build a business that serves your customers, serves your team, and serves you. That's the win/win/win scenario that we look at when building businesses.

To drive towards both your business and life goals, we want to piece together the rest of your business around the engine so that it becomes a fully functioning vehicle. Just like your engine, your vehicle will not start out as a high-end supercar. Instead, it will likely start out as a starter car. Over time, you will be able to upgrade various pieces of the vehicle as your business grows.

THE ENGINE & THE CAR

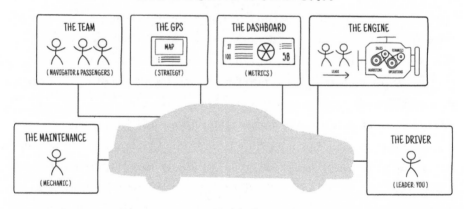

Adding the rest of the parts to your business.

When you have a vehicle engine that is tuned, the vehicle can move. When your business engine is tuned, the business will move. But without having a driver, a destination, regular maintenance, etc., the car will just drive aimlessly and eventually break down. A business is much the same way.

Leadership

When we talk about *people first*, it starts with you as the leader of your business. Most entrepreneurs don't realize or acknowledge that they are the most important person in their business. They started it. They have the vision—with a uniqueness and "unfair advantage" that separates both them and their business from their competitors.

As the leader, you are in control of your business GPS. In order to ensure that the engine moves the vehicle in the right direction, you will be setting the direction—and destination—of the business with your vision/mission. Not only will you be setting it, but you are responsible for designing the engine and vehicle that will get you there. There is a lot on your plate.

This is not to say that you are doing all of this alone. As a leader, you typically want to be spending your time working *on* the business instead of working *in* the business. This means that you are spending less time actually doing the work that the engine should be doing (in the vehicle) and instead are designing and upgrading your business (on the vehicle). Now early on, you are likely doing a lot of the engine work. As your business grows, you want to be intentional about continuing to move this work off of your plate.

How do you do this? You build off the core processes of each area of your engine that we introduced in the previous chapter. Every week you will have reflection/planning meetings where you will look at wins and challenges from the prior seven days and plan out your upcoming week. When challenges present themselves, they are opportunities to improve an area/process. When you plan the upcoming week, identify the gap in the process that's challenging your business and update it to close the gap. You should use the six-step process of creating, analyzing, eliminating, consolidating, automating and delegating for this.

By doing this, you will first reduce the amount of time that you spend doing this engine work, then you will get it off your plate by having either technology or a person take care of it. This will in turn free your time and energy up to focus on building the vehicle. You will be able to set direction, monitor progress, determine when pieces of the vehicle require upgrades, etc.

While this is not a book on leadership, it *is* a book on leadership skills. By starting a business, you are choosing to be a leader, deciding what you want your business to look like to achieve your Ideal Everyday Experience. When you choose to make an improvement in your life and start a business, whether you realize it or not, you are choosing to go on a journey of personal development. You are choosing to look inside and get to know yourself more than you ever have. This journey will test you. It will throw various challenges at you. In order to succeed, you need to continuously work on improving yourself. This mindset of always making things better is critical.

As your business grows, you will continually be forced to *level up* as a leader. Tom spent many years working with leaders in a wide range of companies—from single-person startups through billion-dollar corporations. The common theme in the successful leaders and businesses was that they had the emotional intelligence to realize they needed to continually *level up* and seek out the support and guidance they needed to navigate each of new level.

Let's take the example of kids. When they are born, they can't do much and must rely on someone else to carry them around. In time, they learn to move their bodies and begin rolling. Soon after, they begin crawling. This works much better than rolling, so they spend more of their time crawling and less time rolling. Then they eventually figure out how to walk. This is amazing! At this point, they abandon crawling and start walking everywhere (better babyproof that house!). Then they learn to run. The key is that each time they grew with how they moved, they had to reduce or even let go of the movement that got them to that point. This is one of the biggest challenges leaders face, and it's what keeps them and their businesses stuck. When they are unable to let go of what got them here, they hold themselves back from getting ahead.

Another challenge that can come up and sabotage your leadership ability is ego. Your ego, your feeling of self-esteem or importance, will be required at times in this journey to push you through some of those challenges. At the same time, it will also hold you back.

Tom encountered this first hand as a business consultant. He was often much younger than the business leaders he worked with and, at times, felt intimidated. He would fear looking dumb or getting kicked out of a company for giving real feedback on where the problems were or what needed to change. This caused Tom not to do everything he could to help his clients. He wouldn't ask the "dumb" questions for fear of being embarrassed. He wouldn't provide the much-needed feedback for fear of upsetting the leader and potentially losing business. As a result, he hurt these clients by refraining from doing the job he was hired to do.

This was when a mentor of Tom's stepped in. (*Note: Successful people almost always have mentors, coaches and other people around them to support them. It's not a sign of weakness, but a sign of strength.*) After hearing some of Tom's struggles, he said point blank, "It's not about you." Tom was confused, so he continued. "Your clients have hired you because they have a problem, and they believe you can help them solve it. This is not about you, but about how you can help them. When you agreed to work with them, you agreed to do everything in your power to help them. If you are holding back because you are afraid, that's your problem to deal with, not theirs. So, quit making this about you and make it all about them."

That changed everything. Tom started asking the tough questions. He began providing the tough feedback. He would be himself and unconventional. He became known for his passion in serving, and all of Tom's clients knew that he always needed a whiteboard around so that they could collaboratively solve problems as they came up.

We didn't truly realize the power of this until Tom had one of his normal weekly meetings with a vice president of a large financial company. As he entered her office, she said:

"Tom, you know, you are really good at getting naked."

As you could imagine, Tom just sat there for a few moments, not really sure what to say. The woman let Tom sit uncomfortably for several moments before she added, "I just finished reading this book called *Getting Naked*. It focuses on why some consultants are amazing and why others suck. The ones who are amazing are good at getting naked, which is why we all love you."

After this interaction, of course Tom picked the book up to read on his flight home. After reading it, Tom finally began to understand why his methods worked so well, even though they were unconventional and dramatically different than what he saw most other consultants do. The book outlined the Naked Service Model[7] and the three fears that sabotage client loyalty:

- **Fear of Losing the Business:** This drives a service provider to protect their client base, business opportunities and revenue by censoring feedback and avoiding difficult issues.

- **Fear of Being Embarrassed:** This impedes a service provider's ability to provide open, honest insights because they hold back their ideas, hide their mistakes and edit themselves to save face.
- **Fear of Feeling Inferior:** This challenges a service provider's assumption that they must preserve their social standing with the client at all costs.

Even though *Getting Naked* focused on service providers, it was really a book about the core leadership qualities of being honest, vulnerable and serving the people around you. These are tough but necessary lessons to go through as you grow as a leader. For more insights on leadership, head over to lifestylebuildersbook.com.

Strategy

Strategy is one of those words that you often hear people say, but if you were to ask them their definition, they may struggle to articulate what it actually is. You will also likely walk away with many different definitions of strategy. So, for the context of this discussion, we will use Patrick Lencioni's definition of strategy[8].

Strategy: The collection of intentional decisions an organization makes to give itself the best chance to succeed and differentiate from competitors.

When Tom first heard this definition, it took him a little by surprise. He had struggled to define what he actually meant when he said it, and this definition was not only simple, but the most down-to-earth definition that we had come across. It took this pie-in-the-sky idea of creating your overall business strategy and boiled it down to a set of intentional decisions to guide you.

Intentional is the key word there. Without it, you leave your decisions up to the current tide of your business, industry, personal life or feelings. This is dangerous, as it is very easy to make knee-jerk decisions that won't get you to your goal—and could destroy your business.

Going back to our discussion about your business vehicle: If you are driving the car but not really sure where you are going or the path to get there, you are likely to make last second turns and potentially go down a bunch of different roads that are not in line with your destination and won't get you where you want to go. That is why when you enter your destination into the GPS, it then maps out a potential path to get there. This path lists the roads and milestones that you should expect to encounter along the way. As a result, you are not taking random turns and detours leaving your passengers and other cars on the road confused. Your GPS is guiding you, letting you know when a turn is coming up so that you and your team can anticipate it and move as one.

This is often a challenge with leaders—especially entrepreneurs. As entrepreneurs, we have grand visions and move fast. Sometimes we struggle to articulate those visions and often don't take the time to document and share them with others. This causes those around us to feel more like anchors holding us back, rather than boosters rocketing us forward. Its often why entrepreneurs get to a point where they question if they should even have other people involved, or if it would just be easier to do everything themselves. Their perspective is that it is a problem with the people around them, not being aware that the real problem is them not defining and communicating the strategy to those around them.

As the leader in your business, it is your responsibility to have an overall strategy. That is, a set of intentional decisions that will guide you and those around you forward. In Section 1 of this book, we introduced the Life Planner to help you define and articulate where you wanted your life to go and some principles that would guide you on that journey. We use a similar concept to do the same thing with your business (you can grab a copy of our Business Planner template at www.lifestylebuildersbook.com).

In Section 3 (Concept to Cash), we introduced you to a one-page business plan called a Lean Canvas. That business plan is great to get your business started, but it lacks some of what's needed to provide true direction and guidance to a business as they move forward. This business planner is a tool that you can use to fill that gap.

The first page covers the high-level information of your business's identity and purpose, as well as some mid- and long-terms goals. Some of this will come from the work that you've done with your Lean Canvas. Your business's identity is focused on the business and helps other understand its vision and values. This helps attract the right people, be it team members or customers. The vision is focused on who the business helps and how. The Five-Year Targets and Three-Years Targets help get everyone aligned on where the business is going and how fast.

We also see One-Year Goals and a breakdown by quarter. This helps the business to hone in on the short term and, just like with the Life Planner, builds a roadmap to the longer term goals.

As we discussed in Section 1 (Plan With Purpose), these goals should be written in the format "From <where you are> to <where you want to be> by <when>". In this example, the timeframe is set because it is quarterly (every 90 days). So, the focus is defining which goals you want to focus on for each 90-day chunk to achieve your One-Year Goals. The more you can limit and focus your goals, the easier it will be to achieve them. If you attempt to split the focus across many goals, each one will move forward more slowly. The beauty of this sheet is it is a simple and consolidated place to see the business's current status as well as where it is going.

Once you have goals defined, you want to further break these goals down so that you can plan, execute and achieve them within the next 90 days. For each goal, you want to consider additional criteria as you break it down, such as:

- Owner
- How much revenue it should generate and what percentage of your overall revenue this goal contributes
- The marketing and sales process, along with key metrics to track
- Key actions (projects and tasks) required to achieve the goal, along with milestones to achieve along the way
- The people who will be required
- Mindsets and disciplines required
- Enablers who will help you achieve this goal and barriers that will get in the way
- Educational and technology needs

By going through this activity, you will get your thoughts about the business down on paper. It will force you to articulate where you are, where you want to go and how you plan to get there. It will also allow those around you to understand so they can support you on the journey.

Here are a few additional tips to help you succeed with this:

- **Focus on Revenue Goals First:** Whether or not you are motivated by money, money is a scorecard and will help you achieve both your business and life goals. Most people are not motivated directly by money, but by what money will allow them to do. Either way, your first goals should be directly related to the revenue that you want to generate. Each goal should indicate if it is revenue generating or not. Be sure that when you finish your planning, you know how you plan to generate each dollar of your revenue.

- **Limit Non-Revenue Goals:** Although it is fine to have goals that don't directly contribute to revenue, limit how many of these you have and make sure you first focus on your revenue goals. Non-revenue goals should be focused on supporting revenue goals, like hiring additional people, improving a process to be more efficient, etc.

- **Don't Confuse Projects for Goals:** Often times when we review people's goals, what we find is a list of projects. A goal is the end result that you want to achieve. This is why we recommend the format defined above (from x to y by z), which will help you make sure you are focusing on the end results. Projects are the steps that you will take to achieve your *end results goal.* To get to the end results goal, take a goal that you have defined and ask "why." *Why do you want to update your website?* Maybe you are looking to improve the conversion rate so that you can get more sales? The end result goal would be improving website sales from x to y, and one of the key actions/ projects would be to update the website to resolve bottlenecks in the purchasing process.

- **Establish These Goals "Offsite":** Businesses typically get of out of the office to do planning every 90 days (we will discuss this more in a bit). When you are initially setting, and later on updating, these goals, find a location somewhere other than your normal working location. Not only does this help reduce distractions and temptations to dive into your regular work, but it also gets you in a different state of mind that is better for planning. If you have a team, invite your leaders. If it is just you, consider pairing up with another business owner and helping each other with planning. Simply talking and collaborating with someone else can bring insights, breakthroughs and accountability.

People

We've mentioned *your team* a few times thus far. If the business is just you at this point, then you are the team. As your business grows, you will start replacing yourself with other people so that you don't get overwhelmed and can focus on the activities where you provide the most value.

To keep your vehicle running smooth as it grows, you need a team of people. Someone needs to set the course and destination. Someone needs to drive it. Someone needs to fill it with gas. Someone needs to clean it. Someone needs to perform maintenance on it and fix it when it has an issue or break down. Now you may be able to do all of these tasks yourself but is likely not the best use of your time.

Each of us has a Zone of Genius. That is when you are in the flow; you enjoy what you are doing, you excel at it, no one else can do what you do, and it is highly valuable. You want to identify this and spend more of your time there. There will be many tasks that fall outside of your Zone of Genius, and it doesn't benefit you, your business, your team or your customers to try and perform these tasks. Not only do you likely not enjoy them, you are likely not that great at them either, and you get paid more for work in your Zone of Genius that you do for them. If these tasks are taking you away from your Zone of Genius, that is not good, as no one else can do those Zone of Genius tasks, so less of them are getting done.

This is the trap that many struggling business owners fall into. They take on all of the work themselves. This typically means that not only are you are likely not getting paid if you are not working, but you also are splitting your time over a variety of activities that range in value, expertise, and your Zone of Genius. One hour you may be doing sales activities, which may be a $500/hour activity. The next, you are handling customer support, which may be a $15/hour activity. From this example, it's clear that you should be spending more of your time doing your sales activities and less on your customer support activities, because you make more money doing sales activities. Ironically, as you generate more sales, the need to handle customer support will increase, drawing your time away from high-value activities and into low-value ones. This is where many businesses hit growth plateaus, and business owners start to burnout.

The solution to this is not to try and be superman and do everything yourself, but to build your own team of super heroes. Your super heroes will have their own strengths and uniqueness, while being aligned and committed to the mission, core values, vision and goals of the business. This goes back to what we discussed earlier about being a leader. As the leader of your business, you are in control of its destination and design. As your business grows, you will need to evaluate where the focus of the business, and your time, should be. Your role will be changing often. You will always have the lead in the direction and design of the business, but you want to constantly take things that are not in your Zone of Genius off your plate.

Earlier we introduced a six-step method for creating an optimizing your processes. These steps include creating, analyzing, eliminating, consolidating, automating and delegating. We also introduced the pieces of your business engine (marketing, sales, operations and finance), along with a starting set of high-level processes for each. As you build your business engine, you will be working on expanding and optimizing these processes.

You may have heard people mention working *in* your business versus *on* your business. This means doing the work versus designing the work. Early on you may very well be doing all of the work in your engine—doing marketing, doing sales, doing operations and doing finance. This is OK to start, but definitely not where you want to stay. As you move forward, you will use the six-step optimization process to further create and optimize each component of your engine. By doing this, not only will you make your engine more effective and efficient, but you will also get to the point where you can begin delegating some of these tasks. That means that you will spend less time working *in* your business (doing the engine work) and more time working *on* your business (designing and upgrading the engine and the vehicle). Ultimately, you want to get to a point where you can step away for extended periods of time and still have the business running without you.

In order to do this, you need to build a team. Depending on your specific goals and business, this may be a small team, employing just a few contractors. If you have grander ambitions, it may be a larger team that also includes employees. Either way, the process is the same. You define the core processes of your engine, manage the business via a handful of key metrics on your dashboard (more on this below) and use that to continually refine where you need to focus, what you need to get off your plate and who you need to hire next to delegate things to.

As you go to hire people, it is critical to hire the *right* people—people who believe in your mission and share your core values (both defined on your business planner). Yes, their skills and experience are important too, but far too often people weight skills far more than fitting into the company, which causes more management issues down the line. You are looking for people who you can work with and those who you don't have to motivate, because they are motivated by your mission and want to be a part of your company. The reason that you are hiring people is to make your life easier, not more difficult. So just like you identified your ideal client, spend some time identifying your ideal team member and use that as a criterion when hiring.

Cadence

We discussed setting your goals in the strategy section above. Settings goals is important, but what may be more important is keeping you and your team aligned as you execute towards the goals (and pivoting when needed).

To do this, you need to establish a cadence/routine for when you will check-in, what information you need and how you will decide where to focus. This is where your cadence comes in.

You were already introduced to it, believe it or not. In chapter 1.4 (Create Your Process), you established a set of check-in points for realigning on your personal roadmap. As a refresher, those checkpoints were annually (once a year), quarterly (once every 90 days), monthly, weekly, and daily. This is the same cadence that you will use for your business, which is nice because it keeps things consistent between your life and business.

We previously talked about working *in the business* versus *on the business*. When it comes to you cadence, your meetings are grouped into these two buckets. The *in the business* meetings are your daily and weekly meetings. In these meetings, you and your team align and reflect on what has been done and what needs to be done to achieve the goals.

The *on the business* meetings are then the monthly, quarterly, and annual meetings. These meetings step away from the day-to-day activities and focus on the big-picture planning. During these meetings, you are reviewing goal progress and metrics, reflecting on past progress, and updating goals and direction of the company.

Many businesses struggle because they don't establish a cadence early on. In an ideal structure, you are spending about 10% of your time with these meetings. Most people see meetings as a waste of time because of poor experiences in their past. The reality is that most people don't know how to effectively set and run meetings. They are often avoiding implementing a cadence like this one yet will then have a bunch of ad-hoc meetings because they didn't spend enough time planning and updating. Below is a breakdown of the cadence and how much time it will take you throughout the course of a year.

Meeting	Frequency	Meeting Length	Total Time (Year)
Annual	Once a year	2 Days	16 Hours
Quarterly	Once a quarter	1 Day	24 Hours
Monthly	Once a month	½ Day	44 Hours
Weekly	Once a week	90 Minutes	40 Hours
Daily	Once a day	15 Minutes	65 Hours
		Total Meeting Time (Year):	**189 Hours**

There are 2,080 hours in a year (assuming 52 weeks a year * 40 hours a week). Now you may not work all 52 weeks, but you likely are not just working 40 hours a week either, so it all works out.

So 189 hours for meetings / 2,080 working hours available = ~9%. Add 1% more for admin/context switching, and it only comes out to 10% of your total time, which is not a lot. That leaves 90% (1,872 hours) available for you to do the work.

So, what do you get in exchange for giving up 10% of your time for these meetings?

- Clarity
- Focus
- Reflection
- Alignment

What these meetings do is to help you define the vision of where you are going, establish a roadmap to get there, allow time to check-in and adjust when you get off, and get you and your team focused on the most important tasks. With all of this working, you will gain back much more than the 10% of time you spend.

Start implementing this cadence today, even if it is just you. Get out your calendar and start blocking off time for each of these meetings. Below are summaries of each meeting, along with a starting point for length. You can adjust based on your needs. If you adjust, be sure to adjust to less time, not more. If you can't complete everything you need in the timeframe provided, focus on improving your processes so you can. Planning is important, but you don't want to spend more time than needed on planning.

Here's what *the business meetings* should consist of:

- **Daily** - 15 minutes or fewer, typically in the morning. Same time, same place. Focus on syncing up and aligning on what was completed yesterday, what your intention/commitment is for today, and what's getting in the way of progress.
- **Weekly** - 90 minutes, typically at the start/end of the week, but mid-week works really well also to avoid vacations and long weekends. Reflect on the prior week, decide what improvements to make, review key metrics, solve tactical issues, and plan the focus/tasks for the upcoming week.
- **Monthly** - 4 hours, near the end of the month. Reflect on 90-day goals, make adjustments to plan/actions based on progress, set upcoming month cash-flow plan and work on solving bigger strategic issues.
- **Quarterly** - 1 day, near the end of the quarter, typically outside of your normal office. Reflect on the previous quarter and plan the upcoming quarter. This is also a great opportunity for some team relationship building.
- **Annually** - 2 days, near the end of the year, or mid-year, which avoids the business of the end of the year. This is should be outside your normal office. Reflect on prior year, review goal completion, update vision/roadmap, and set upcoming year focus/goals. Like the quarterly, this is also a great team-building opportunity.

With a cadence like this established, it will build the foundational routines and habits to create a high-performance business vehicle.

Dashboard

There are a lot of things that we could focus on at any point in time. Our environments have so much going on every second that we couldn't process everything even if we tried. So our brains are designed to filter out information and block anything it believes isn't important. There is a great video that shows this perfectly. The video has a small group of people, half wearing black shirts and half wearing white shirts. It asks you to count the number of times people with white shirts pass the ball over the course of a minute. If you haven't seen this video, before reading on, go to our resources page at lifestylebuildersbook.com and find: "Daniel Simons and Christopher Chabris Selective Attentiveness."

Go watch the video before proceeding! The next paragraph contains a spoiler alert.

After some time has passed, the video reveals the correct answer, and asks you if you saw the gorilla. At this point, most people say, "What gorilla?" The video rewinds, and low and behold, a black gorilla walks right through the middle of the people passing the balls around, waves his hands, and continues walking out of the screen. This is not a camera trick, the gorilla was in the video the first time you watched it, but you brain filtered it out because you were focused on counting the number of passes by people with white shirts. Since this gorilla was not wearing a white shirt and wasn't passing a ball, you missed it.

The same thing can easily happen in other areas of your business and life. What we give our attention to is typically what we see. It's just like the example of when you buy a new car and suddenly you begin seeing that car everywhere. It's not that there weren't other people driving that car before, but now you are aware.

Driving your business vehicle will cause you to experience much of the same. There is so much information that it can easily become overwhelming. Your brain will do its best to filter things out, but without you being intentional and telling it what to focus on, you could miss big issues or opportunities that were there all along because you were focusing on something else.

How can you possibly keep track of everything? The simple answer is that you don't, and you don't need to. The key to keeping your vehicle running smooth is to keep track of a handful of important information, which conveniently is stored right in front of you as you drive. It's called your *dashboard*.

The dashboard in your car tells key information about your car, from information about how it is currently operating, such as speed and direction, to warnings to potential problems, such as engine overheating or low tire pressure. In effect what it does is allow you to sit comfortably in the driver's seat, while at the same time informing you of the key information that you need to be aware of as you drive. Your business vehicle should be no different. It is in front of you at all times and informs you as to how the business is running. Many entrepreneurs struggle because they don't have a dashboard for their business. It would be like driving your car without your dashboard. You wouldn't know which direction you are going, how fast you are going, if you are low on fuel, if issues are creeping up, etc. When you don't know what's going on, you get into poor practices, like thinking that you need to be involved in every aspect of your business, leading to long hours that will overwhelm you. Or you struggle to get to important tasks done because it seems like new urgent issues pop up all the time, pulling you away from your Zone of Genius.

When you implement a dashboard for your business, what you are doing is giving yourself one go-to place to get a feel for how things are progressing, as well as a place to be alerted to potential issues before they become large and urgent issues. This allows you to focus where you need to, while keeping a pulse on the business and avoiding the dreaded micromanagement of employees.

Now that you know you need a dashboard, what should you put on it? As you look around, there are no shortage of information and metrics available to you. You could easily have hundreds (or thousands) of pieces of data (metrics) on your dashboard. This would not help you though, as it will become overwhelming and make you miss important information because it is buried between all the less important information (just like the gorilla). So, what you want to focus on are called *Key Performance Indicators* (KPIs).

Every business is different, and just about every business dashboard is different. The key to developing a dashboard for your business is to start with some common KPIs, then adjust it as you refine what information is critical for you to lead your business and avoid issues. Luckily, you have an easy place to start, which is your engine and the high-level processes that you've created for each piece.

If you remember, the 4 components of your engine are marketing, sales, operations and finance. Each of these had a high-level process with three to five steps. So, your starting dashboard can be organized around these components and steps. Each component can have two to three key pieces of information for how that component is doing. A few potentials are below:

Marketing

- **Number of New Leads** – How many potential customers take the first action? This could be sending you a message, giving you their contact information, or coming into your store.

- **Number of New Prospects** – How many people take the next action in your process, indicating that they are potentially interested in a purchase? This could be completing an application, requesting a proposal, or inquiring about a purchase.

Sales

- **Number of Sales Activities** – How many prospects move onto your sales activity? This could be having a sales call/presentation, visiting a sales website, or adding an item to their cart.

- **Number of New Customers** – How many prospects made a purchase? This could be the number of new customers and/or revenue collected.

Operations

- **Number of Satisfied Customers** – How many customers are happy with their experience after purchasing? This may be measured via a question/survey or via how many people stay a customer and don't leave/request a refund.

- **Number of Repeat Purchases** – How many customers return and purchase again? This may be measured via churn rate or people that make an additional purchase.

Finance

- **Profit First Breakdown** - A breakdown of how the cash that you have is bucketed in each account. This can be measured by what percent of your revenue you are moving to each account.

- **Cash Collected** – The amount of money that you collect. This can be measured as a percent compared to what you sold.

Here are some additional things to consider when developing your business dashboard.

- **Dashboards Highlight Data, But Rarely Provide Answers**: The purpose of your dashboard is to allow you to keep a pulse on the business and help you determine where to focus your attention. Just like an indicator informing you that you tire pressure is low doesn't tell you why, your dashboard metrics will highlight issues, but will require you to dive in deeper to understand why and what you action you should take as a result.

- **They Should Be Accurate:** The only thing worse than not having a dashboard is having one that you believe is correct but isn't. If you are operating off of incorrect data, you will make poor business decisions. Automate whatever data gathering you can on your dashboard and have a process/person in place to update the remaining items.

- **They Should Be Valuable:** Even though you may start with some common metrics or use dashboards from other businesses for inspiration, your dashboard should be customized to your business and be useful. Regularly review what metrics are useful to act on versus the ones that aren't and evolve your dashboard accordingly.

- **They Will Evolve:** Your dashboard should change over time to reflect the phase of business you are in. When you just start, you will likely track things relating to validating your idea, such as number of customer interviews held, hypothesis tested, and potential early adopters. Later your dashboard will evolve to contain key information about your goal progress and each engine component, such as the number of sales and total revenue.

- **They Should Be Easily Accessible/Visible:** You want to be able to see it often. Ideally, your dashboard is in your face so that you can see changes and use it to help guide your decisions. This may be on a physical white board or wall, or electronically and displayed on a screen on the wall. Either way, make it visible so that you look at it often, especially during each of your cadence meetings. Also, utilizing graphs and other visuals often makes them easier to read/comprehend as compared to just straight numbers.

- **Don't Overcomplicate It:** The key thing is to get started. Pick a few metrics that you believe are important to review and start tracking them. This may be as simple as how much revenue was generated the week before. Once you start, you will then find gaps in your dashboard information and you can evolve it. Also, don't let finding a tool or automating your dashboard get in the way. Start manually with a simple whiteboard or spreadsheet. We've worked with businesses generating millions and hundreds of millions a year that are using simple spreadsheets. Keep it simple until it makes sense to move on to something bigger.

Section 5:
Quit Your Cubicle

Section Summary:

With a lot of hard work, some pivots along the way, and a little bit of luck, your business will grow to a point where you achieve your freedom number and can leave your job. This is an awesome time in your life, but it comes with some new shifts and challenges as you transition from an employee to a full-time entrepreneur.

The goal of this section is to help you to make the transition as seamless and possible and help you navigate through some of the challenges that will arise as you make the transition.

Are We Really Doing This?

Tom's Take

I had just returned from a business conference. Ariana and I typically attend a handful of conferences each year. Part of it is to keep learning, part of it is building new connections and meeting new people, part of it is to speak to help others, part of it is being able to travel and see new places while also moving our businesses forward. It's a pretty good setup.

I was on a conference call with the consulting company that I worked for at the time.

"Tom, we need to move you from salary to hourly."

I had worked as a consultant for this company for a little more than a year and had finished up a contract with a client several months before. This company was trying to grow this new department as a new service offering, but it had been a challenge. I spent more of my time directly working with clients, which were often large corporations that were looking to improve the efficiency and effectiveness of their IT departments developing software products for the company. That didn't leave me much time to develop this new product line, especially considering that it was starting a new business inside an existing one.

Prior to working with this company, I had been doing business consulting for about 4 years. During this time, I gained so much experience. I worked with top business leaders and executives, who brought me in to help them develop their products and make their teams more efficient. But often I would end up coaching their leaders and helping them develop and implement their business strategy so that they could benefit from the improved team effectiveness and new product development process. I was getting the opportunity to speak, to train, to facilitate company offsites and to help not only the businesses, but the people who worked for them. It was amazing, except for the fact that it took a lot of time and took me away from my family. I was traveling 4-5 days a week. The clients whom I worked with were located across the United States. My weekly routine consisted of spending half of my day Sunday ironing and packing my luggage for the week. I also had to mentally prepare to be away from my family again, which was difficult as I had only gotten back two days prior.

My alarm would go off at 4 A.M. on Monday morning, though I generally had trouble sleeping the night before leaving, so I'd be awake before it rang. I would head to the airport and fly to whatever city needed me. I would land, check in to my hotel (which I accidentally called my home on numerous occasions) and head into work. I spent more time with these clients and in these cities than I did with my family.

My schedule was working Monday through Thursday at the client's location, leaving Thursday afternoon or evening to fly back home (assuming my flight didn't get delayed or cancelled). That meant I had to get my 40-plus hours in over the course of 3 ½ to 4 days, working 10-12 hour shifts with clients, not including travel time to get there and get home.

After work, I would grab dinner, head to the hotel and work on our entrepreneur coaching business at night in the hotel room. I rarely went out and explored the cities. I couldn't enjoy it without Ariana and the kids were at home and missing out.

When Thursday night rolled around, I would head to the airport and hope that I got home before my kids went to bed. On the weeks when this did happen, a rush of emotions would come over me as I flew home. I was so excited to see my daughter standing at the waiting area of the airport, going crazy when she saw me. She would check my luggage for a "friend" (a Beanie Boo—this little stuffed animal that all the airport stores sold to travelers like me). After finding it, she would hug it tight and guide me over to the escalator. We would go up and down it a few times, and she perfected her timing of leaping off the escalator right before we got to the end. This was a game, and she loved it!

Our daughter was 2 when I first started my position as a traveling business consultant. During that time Ariana gave birth to our son. I loved squeezing my wife when I got to see her each week. It reminded me how lucky I was to be building this life with her. But it also made me extremely sad and filled with anxiety, knowing that in a few days she would go back to being a single mom to two young children when I flew out to my second home.

So, when my boss said to me, "Tom, we need to move you from salary to hourly," I knew this was an opportunity to leave, free up for time for my family, as well as time to grow our coaching businesses and create a bigger impact for entrepreneurs like us. But I was still nearly a year away from having the financial flexibility to leave this job to run our 3 companies full time. The challenge became trying to make the responsible decision as I had a wife and two children to consider.

Ariana's Take:

"You need to tell them you're done. This is ridiculous."

I'm not sure if those were my exact words, but pretty darn close. I had watched Tom struggle with his job as a consultant for years. I knew how much it took out of him to leave us every Monday and return home Thursday after missing four out of seven days with his family. It didn't help his job was highly stressful. Honestly, I was so done with all of it—the travel, me being a single mom for half the year— that when they gave him that line of bull about "wanting to see if he was dedicated to making the program work" and dropping him down to an hourly position (in which we would lose our benefits, oh joy!) I did an extremely uncomfortable thing and told my husband to leave his six-figure job.

I was tired—tired of running the household on my own, running our three businesses, raising a three-year-old and breastfeeding an infant who refused to sleep for the first 18 months of his life. Mowing the lawn, paying the bills, groceries, appointments, dishes, laundry, cleaning, bath time, story time, chauffer, chef; the list is endless. And even worse, I knew I had to be strong for Tom when he came home on the weekends, since he was the one missing out and feeling miserable for leaving us every week. I was being all the things to everybody, and I almost lost myself because of it.

Were we ready for a new way of life? Mentally, emotionally and physically, hell yes! Financially? Not so much. We had a runway, but it wasn't quite as long as we had hoped.

Before those three years of our life happened, I would have stood by our plan and said "Nope! We're not ready yet!" But the new Ariana—the one who felt like she had been dragged through the mud and pummeled and still came out of it OK—she was ready for something else. I wanted my husband back. I wanted him happy and not stressed out all the time. I wanted my partner back, so I could stop doing it all as a solo show and we could go back to being a team. Both myself and the kids wanted their dad back, that fun guy they occasionally got to see for a couple days each week, before he took Sunday to prepare, pack and leave us again.

We were presented with a situation, and we could use it as an opportunity instead of seeing it as a failure. This was our chance to start living our ideal life now.

Chapter 5.2

Quitting Day

O ne of the biggest questions that we get from entrepreneurs who have built their business on the side is: When will they hit the tipping point where they can quit their jobs and go all in on their business?

There is not a one size fits all answer for this. In Section 2 (Find Your Freedom), we provided you with the tools to figure out your Freedom Number and your runway. If you remember, your Freedom Number is the amount of money that your business needs to pay you every month in order to cover all of your expenses, including additional expenses that will occur when you leave your job (such as paying for your own health insurance).

In the *ideal* scenario, you don't quit your job until your business is paying you more than your Freedom Number and you are confident that this will continue, because at that point you can cover your monthly expenses without your paycheck. Additionally, you've likely built up a decent savings of at least three-to-six months of expenses because you've had the double income of your paycheck from your job and your paycheck from your business.

With that said, in our experience, very few people actually follow the ideal scenario, including us. Most people leave their jobs before their business is fully paying them their Freedom Number. In this scenario, you need a long runway to provide yourself enough time to build your business income up to a point where you can pay yourself your freedom number each month. If you need a refresher on these concepts, go back and review Chapter 2.4 (Define Your Freedom Number) and Chapter 2.6 (Laying Out Your Runway).

As you get to the point where you are considering leaving and going full time, here are some questions to help you decide if it is the right time:

- **Is Your Business Consistently Growing?** Before you quit, you want to show a track record of (at a minimum) consistent sales, and ideally growing sales. One great month of sales is awesome, but if you can't replicate it, you will struggle. Many entrepreneurs will do a large launch/promotion and see a spike in sales for the month, only to struggle after because they've converted all of their hot prospects into customers but haven't built out their marketing and sales systems to bring in and warm up new leads and prospects.

- **Are You Due Any Bonuses or Will You Owe Anything?** There may be scenarios where if you stayed at a job longer, you may be eligible for additional compensation, which may affect your decision to leave. In other cases, you may have signed a contract saying that you would stay employed for a period of time or you will pay back a portion of your initial bonus, or you may have taken a loan from your retirement account. There are a handful of scenarios in which you could owe money or face a penalty for leaving your employment. Check into these cases to make sure you won't be surprised with bills or fees when you leave.

- **Do You Have a Non-Compete?** Some companies will have their employees sign agreements such as a non-compete. Although each agreement will vary, in general these place limits on developing business relationships with clients and employees of your current employer for a period of time. Review any paperwork that you initially signed as part of your onboarding and make sure you know what you are legally bound to.

- **Have You Lined Up Health Insurance?** Many people are surprised at the cost of health insurance when they leave their jobs. This cost itself keeps many people in their jobs. Be sure to explore and line up health insurance before you leave. COBRA is always an option, but it can cost significantly more than you are aware of, given that your employer may be paying a portion of your health insurance costs currently.

- **Have You Considered All of the Cons?** One of Ariana's favorite ways to make a decision is to make a simple list of pros and cons, then evaluate and decide. When evaluating cons, see if you are comfortable with each of them, and look for opportunities to reduce or mitigate the impact. As much as you can, you want to prepare and avoid unexpected surprises after you leave.

In most cases, you are better off staying at your job for as long as you can. The consistency of a paycheck will reduce your pressure and stress, as well as allow you to build up your savings and build your business the way you want—rather than having to make decisions based on the need for income. More entrepreneurs fail from quitting their jobs too early versus staying at their jobs too long. If you really don't enjoy your job or need more flexibility, look into alternatives, such as seeing if your employer will allow you to drop down to part time work, or if you can become an independent contractor with them.

When you finally decide that it is to leave your job and go all in as an entrepreneur, it is exciting. Congratulations! You've put in a lot of hard work to get to this point, and it is a very exciting (and likely scary) time. Below are some things to consider when you finally make the decision to leave:

- **Don't Burn Bridges:** Even though you have dreams of never working for someone again, you can't see into the future. It's never good to burn bridges, especially when you may want/need to work with your current employer again. Maybe things change and you need a job in the future. Maybe you want to offer your services to your current employer. Maybe your business is in a similar space so you will interact with the same groups of people. Regardless of the reason, you don't want people speaking ill of you. Additionally, how you leave says a lot about you and your character. Leaving during a busy time or without much notice could put your employer in an unnecessary challenging situation. Also, some organizations provide an exit interview, typically with someone from human resources. As tempting as it can be to unload emotions, we recommend leaving on great terms and not throwing blame or leaving negatively.

- **Provide as Much Notice as You Can:** The standard timeframe for notice is two weeks. This should always be followed, but if you can give additional notice, that is sometimes even better. The more advance warning your employer has, the more time they can work on filling the gap you leave and allow you time to train your colleagues to take over your responsibilities. With this approach, just be aware that your employer can choose to let you go before you plan to leave. If you are working for a great company and are a great employee, they will want to get as much out of you before you leave. With that said, be sure that you will be OK if they choose to let you go earlier. Also know that you may be treated differently if people know you are leaving, and it will be tough to reverse course if you change your mind and want to stay.

- **Prepare for the Conversation:** Take some time to prepare for the conversation with your manager. He or she should be the first person that you talk to. Request a meeting and be sure to bring a resignation letter. Know what you will say and be prepared for what conversation may come. You can share information about why you are leaving and your new opportunity, but you don't have to provide details. You can simply say that it is a great opportunity you can't pass up. Also, make sure you have prepared answers for common questions employees who are leaving get asked. What will you say if the boss wants you to stay and offers you more money? What if they want you to stay longer than your notice? Are you prepared if they let you go on the spot and escort you out of the office? Be prepared for each of these scenarios in advance.

- **Look into Transition Programs:** Some government and educational organizations will have grants and support for entrepreneurs and business owners making the transition. You may be eligible for some additional support (financial, educational, resources, etc.) These programs may not be available in all areas and you may not be eligible for them, but it doesn't hurt to spend a little bit of time researching.

- **Look to Reduce Your Expenses:** You want to provide yourself with the greatest opportunity to succeed—especially if you are leaving your job before your business is paying your Freedom Number. Looking for opportunities to lower your Freedom Number can help a lot. For example, we sold off one of our vehicles and opted to replace it with one that was one-third of the cost.

- **Check into Your Credit Needs:** People need credit for various reasons, such as purchasing a house or vehicle. They may also need to take out a business loan. It is much easier to do this when you have a job and can show the bank your W-2 income. Without a W-2, it is much more difficult to get a loan from a bank. If you are considering a major purchase that will require borrowing money, consider doing it before you leave your job, or pushing it off until you can establish a track record of success from your business.

- **Close Things Out:** There may be some close-out activities to complete your separation from the company. If you have a retirement plan with the company, you could leave it with then, but you are often better off to move it to a plan that is separate from the company (often called a roll-over). Also, collect contact information and anything else that you need but won't have access to once you leave.

You've prepared. Now finish strong and close out this chapter of your life strong so that you can begin the next chapter, not as an employee, but as a full-time entrepreneur.

Settling in as a Full-Time Entrepreneur

"FREEEDOOMMMMMMM" (Think Mel Gibson in Braveheart.)

That is *probably* how you're going feel your first day as a full-time entrepreneur. It may very well be one of the best days of your life! No more J-O-B telling you what to do and how to do it. No alarm clocks, no more sitting in rush-hour traffic, or dealing with that one annoying co-worker. No more company politics. You get to sit at home (in your sweatpants if you're like Ariana) or your new office and work on your business, something that you enjoy! You get to make your own schedule, set your own hours, and be *the boss*.

A couple important things to get you started on the right foot with your new status:

- **Find Your Workspace!** Yes, we know the beauty of the "laptop lifestyle" is that you can literally work from wherever you want. But if you work at home every day, it has a tendency to become monotonous, and that can be a killer for productivity. Also, without a dedicated work area, it can be a challenge to have everything you need to focus. Set yourself up with a space in your home where you can "get in the zone"—an office if you have room, or a desk where you know you can focus. If you find you still have trouble feeling productive at home, don't be afraid to branch out. Hit up your local library/coffee shops, or even a co-working space to shake things up and get out of your norm.

- **Establish Your Routine.** Part of the fun of being a full-time entrepreneur means you can work whenever you want and don't *have* to follow a set schedule. But many people find that without a routine and accountability of a job/boss, the pendulum swings too far the other way. They are busy all the time but rarely get anything done. Or they don't have lines between work and business, so it bleeds together too much not allowing full focus on either. So, one of the best things you can do to set yourself up for success is to establish a routine. That can be as simple as waking up, taking a shower, having your coffee with breakfast, and then sitting down to work for the day. Or, it may be more complex, like Tom's (he gets up earlier than the kids, hydrates, meditates, reads, works out, showers, has his coffee, checks his calendar, fills out his daily planner, meets with Ariana, and then goes to his desk and works with his designated focus music). Find a routine that works for you, and you'll be amazed how much more you get done.

- **Have a Plan.** More time doesn't automatically mean more gets done. This is where that whole "work smarter not harder" mantra comes in. Now that you've got what seems like endless time to do your work and grow your business, make sure you're working towards something. That comes with having a plan with set goals (as we discussed in Chapter 1), so you know what you're working on when you sit down at your workspace. Nothing worse than feeling busy all the time and not seeing that needle move forward.

With those notes considered, let's now discuss what you can *really* expect as you go through this major change.

The Emotional Rollercoaster

One thing that people often fail to anticipate when they leave their job is the emotional rollercoaster that comes along with it. When you give your notice, you may have nervousness and anxiety. When you walk out of the company building for the last time, you will encounter a new level of freedom and excitement. On your first day as a full-time entrepreneur, you will probably wake up early, throw on a pot of coffee and dive right in (unless you are the smash-your-alarm-clock-and-be-glad-that-you-never-have-to-set-it-again type).

As you make the transition, you will experience a series of different emotions. This is normal. Also know that you don't have to—and shouldn't—go through this alone. Be sure to establish some support, specifically people whom you can turn to as you transition. Other entrepreneurs whom you trust and have gone through this transition are typically the best in this case.

Another common but unsuspecting thing that you may encounter is loneliness. If you are used to working somewhere with people, it can be a huge transition to work by yourself or with a smaller team. Things that you took for granted or even loathed (ex. meetings, water cooler chat, etc.) you may come to miss. Again, having other entrepreneurs to support you through this is very helpful. These can be people whom you know and can meet on occasion. It can also be people whom you can connect with online, either in free groups/forums for entrepreneurs or even paid programs. Some people opt to work out of a co-working space, which not only will have you working around other people but may also offer additional support to your business.

Being Your Own Boss

Whether you loved it or hated it, having a boss and working for a company has some perks. When you have a boss, you have someone whom you are accountable to. This person provided you a job description and expectations. If you failed to meet them, he or she let you know, and you had to get back on track.

When you are working for yourself, you are your own boss. Whatever employer issues you experienced in the past are no more. No more micro-management. No more politics. No more people telling you what to do. Those are all great things. But no more people telling you what to do also poses a new challenge: You are now accountable and responsible for *everything*. You are now responsible for all areas of the business, not just your single role. There is no one else to blame. When things go wrong, you have to take full responsibility.

Work/Life Balance

When you had a job, you had work/life/business balance. Now you just have life/business balance, so it should be easier, right? It may be in some cases, but it can also be more challenging, especially if you work from home.

We prefer to discuss work/life "integration" or work/life "harmony." The reality is that striving for balance is often a losing proposition. As time goes on, different things will demand more of your focus and attention. If you have a child, the child will bump up to the top of your list and take a lot of your attention. When you launch your business or have a busy time, that will often take up a larger portion of your time. So instead of trying to balance it all, it's better to look at how you can integrate the various pieces to support each other and create harmony between them all. At some points, some things will become more important to spend your time on, but that doesn't mean you neglect others.

Additionally, many entrepreneurs actually work more than they did at a job. This is due to multiple reasons—they enjoy what they do, they are playing many roles in their business, it takes time to build the business and they have a limited runway, etc. Often times when people have jobs, they despise their job and only show up because they need a paycheck. They get through the week and live for the weekend. Entrepreneurs, while they also need to make money, are typically motivated by being able to create their own thing and to make an impact on not only their clients, but beyond. This means that they enjoy what they do and often want to spend more time doing it.

It's Easy to Neglect Yourself (And Your Health)

Related to the often lack of routines and accountability, coupled with the typical long hours, it's not uncommon for entrepreneurs to neglect taking care of their health—from not drinking enough water, to not getting enough sleep, to eating poorly and not exercising, and also not carving out time for hobbies and activities that you enjoy. As they say when you fly, "please put your oxygen mask on first before helping others." Taking care of yourself, both physically and emotional, should be priority Number One. If you neglect yourself, you will not be able to show up and perform for those most important to you in your life, as well as your business.

Friends and Family

One thing that many entrepreneurs are not prepared for is the response of friends and family as they make changes in their lives. You would think it should be similar to saying, "Oh hey, I got a new job," and they would congratulate you, ask about it with some small talk, and everyone would move forward.

Wrong. When you tell your friends and family that you are starting a business/quitting your job, etc., you will often be met with confusion, questions, concerns and negativity. For the most part, these reactions will be for one of the following reasons:

- **They Are Jealous:** It takes a lot of courage and personal development to not only build a business, but to get to a point where you leave your job and go all in with it. Many people dream of being able to start a business, leave their job and build a life of freedom. At the same time, few people want to put in the work required to make it a reality, and therefore get jealous when they see others able to face their own fears and go after their dreams when they are not willing to do the same. As you start to find success and have some growth, you may have family and friends who use every opportunity to call out your mistakes and failures and use these as reasons you should give up. As much as it hurts to hear this stuff, remember these things reflect more about them and their own internal feelings about themselves than they do about you.

- **They Are Concerned:** While many reactions may come from jealousy, they do not all stem from that. In many cases, especially with those closest to you, they may be looking out for what they believe is your own good. Most people have a fear around business and entrepreneurship, often hearing stats about how many businesses fail. Being an employee themselves and likely someone who hasn't taken the leap into entrepreneurship and never will, they are just trying to look out for your well-being. They see entrepreneurship as being unstable and risky, even though traditional nine-to-five jobs can be just as much so.

- **They Don't Understand Your Choice:** Many people are not entrepreneurs and will never be entrepreneurs. They are content with the traditional path and may not have a drive beyond the life that they have. This is OK. Entrepreneurs are wired differently. Many of your friends and family may not understand your choices to work longer hours in order to build your business, or sell & downsize your house or car in order to give you more options around your income.

- **They Will Think You Are Free All Day/Night:** With not having a traditional schedule, you may find people thinking you are available at all hours of the day to help them. Especially if you work from home, they will just assume that you are free. Or, because you make your own schedule, you are available whenever they want you to be. You can meet me for coffee every Friday morning, right? Or on a random Tuesday afternoon for a movie date. Don't be surprised when you have to explain it (more than once) why this is not the case. Creating a consistent schedule and sharing it with them can help.

- **They Resent Your Choices on Where You Spend Your Time:** When you've decided to go all in on building a business, it is going to take up *a lot* of your time. Whether you're building it on the side while you still have a job or jumping into it after a stint as a stay-at-home parent, you will have fewer hours in the day than you did before. And that time has to be taken away from somewhere. Friends and family are going to start noticing when you have to turn down invitations for social events, or when you can't take their calls. Your spouse will likely have a tough time "sharing" you with your business as well. If your spouse is on board and supportive, great! But he or she is still going to want some personal time with you. If your spouse is not on board with the business, the time you spend on it versus the time you spend with your spouse will definitely become the trigger to many disagreements. Remember to go through the first two sections of this book with your spouse. That will help you get on the same page with why you are starting the business and your financial plan.

Now, being aware of these doesn't mean they go away. You'll likely want to have some ways to combat these issues or handle them. Here are four options:

1. **Be ready to explain *why*** this is important to you as many times as it takes. Talk to them about your dreams and give them examples of other businesses that are doing it.

2. **Ask them for their support.** Say "I don't need you to understand exactly what I'm doing or how it will work, but as someone close to me I could really use your support and trust."

3. **Assure them you will take their concerns to heart.** Sometimes our spouses and close friends can help us find flaws in our plans and point out crucial gaps we didn't see. This is why Ariana had the nickname "reality checker," as she would ask questions and point out details Tom often missed.

4. **Be ready to walk away.** Sometimes, there are going to be people in your life who just don't want you to succeed. It hurts like hell when that happens, especially when it's an immediate family member or a long-time friend. But if you've been doing the first three steps over and over again, and they just aren't getting it or they keep tearing you down and bringing all the negativity, it may be time to walk away. Also, know that once you've found success, these same people may try to find their ways back into your life.

Chapter 5.5

Make Sure You Don't Have To Go Back

O ne of the many unfortunate things that we've seen in our times as entrepreneurs is people leaving their jobs to go all-in on their businesses,
only to have things not work out and have them go back to a regular
job. People declare their freedom, only to have it be a short-lived instead of permanent. This tends to crush the entrepreneur when it happens. Not only does
their ego take a hit, but they've likely burned through a lot of time, money and
energy. Going back to a job takes time away from building the business and can
crush any drive that they once had.

Here are a several things you can do to make sure you stay free from a job.

Manage Your Runway and Cash Flow

In Section 2 (Find Your Freedom), one of the activities that you went through
was mapping out your runway. This was only necessary if your business was not
paying your Freedom Number when you left your job. In this case, you would
have to supplement the gap with savings and continue to increase how much you
pay yourself until it exceeds it.

Every month until you are paying yourself your Freedom Number, you
should be revisiting and updating your runway. This will keep you aware of how
long you have and help direct the actions of your business. For example, if you are
getting short on your runway, that may tell you to shift your focus to spend more
time selling. Staying on top of these numbers will allow you to make adjustments,
as well as avoid surprises when you suddenly can't pay your bills.

Keep Expenses Low

The longer you can keep your expenses low, the better. This goes not only for your personal expenses, but also your business expenses. Target to keep them around 30% of your revenue or less (like we discussed earlier). This will allow you to pay yourself the right percentage, as well as give you money to reinvest back into the business to help it grow.

Build a Buffer/Rainy Day Fund

Although your initial focus is to grow sales and continually increase how much you pay yourselves, it is also important to put some of this money aside for savings. You never know when the unexpected will hit, so it is important to take a portion of your money and start building up a cash reserve (both personally and in your business). This is not only a good habit to develop but will really become useful to get you through some of the rough patches that will come up. This will basically help extend your runway by increasing your savings, rather than depleting it. Once you achieve your Freedom Number, this will help you continue to increase your wealth.

Stick to Your Cadence

The planning and execution cadence are key. By having a consistent cadence of reflecting on what has gone well as well as what's been a challenge, you will stay aware of how you are doing and make adjustments along the way. As we've mentioned a few times, be sure to schedule these in your calendar and focus on sticking to them.

By implementing the above and keeping a pulse on the cash flow of your business (and making adjustments as needed), you can help ensure that you continue to grow your business and keep yourself from having to go back to a job.

Chapter 5.6

Live Your Life

There is absolutely *no* reason you can't start living parts of your ideal life right now. Why do so many of us wait? Why do we think these thoughts of "someday when we have more [time, money, freedom], it would be nice to… [spend time with friends, take the kids on vacation, find a fun hobby]."

The truth is, it's easy to let all of these "would be nice" items get pushed off and dropped down on the priority list. We make excuses as to why we can't do them now—not enough money, not enough time, yada-yada-yada.

BULL. Instead, we want you to start asking *how. How* can you incorporate some of the items on your vision board into your life *now*? Maybe not entirely, but in steps or increments. Take for example, one of our items: Take the kids on a trip to Disney (yes, cliché we know). On our roadmap, this item is a couple years down the road. Instead of waiting *years* to have one single, amazingly fun trip with our kids, we decided to start now!

Introducing - *Friday Family Fun Field Trips!* (We really like alliteration, if you hadn't noticed).

We took Fridays off work for an entire summer, and each week we picked a different fun place to go with the kids. We visited the zoo, the museum, the beach, a local splash park, our state fair, and visited the waterfalls in our award-winning state park! These experiences were really important to us to have with our kids, and we wanted to start living them in whatever capacity we could—even if that just meant short day trips around the area to start.

So, in what ways can you start adding in these mile-markers on your roadmap?

Your Roadmap

Ah, the roadmap. Remember back in Section 1, when you took the items off your vision board and moved them over onto a timeline? This is not one of those things that you create once and then never touch it again. This roadmap is simply a starting point for your journey. It will change and grow as you and your loved ones do. It should not be written in stone, but rather adjusted as you go along. It is a tool to help you as you build your ideal life.

This means you'll need to check in with your roadmap frequently! When you achieve goals, you want to be sure you stop and celebrate. When your goals change, update your roadmap.

Go back and take a look at your roadmap, what items can you take small steps towards now? Maybe one of your goals someday is to buy a bigger house. Obviously, this is a big item, and may be a year (or a few) down the road on your roadmap. What are the reasons you want a bigger house? Do you need more space? Maybe you want some nicer amenities that come with new construction?

We'll throw in an example here, as a bigger house is on our vision board (for both of those above reasons). Last summer we decided the bigger house wouldn't happen for a couple years, so how could we solve the issue of having stuff *all over* our house?! We needed more room but didn't want to build an addition.

Solution: Our kiddos, five years old and two years old at the time, would start sharing a room. Our son's old room would become their playroom, and we would get our living room back! Ariana's parents had bought our daughter a new lofted bed, so when our son graduated to a toddler bed it fit nicely underneath hers. We used three shelves, several foldable bins we had for toy storage, added some new closet shelves and voila! We bought ourselves more space.

Solution #2: Spending a little to create a lot! We also installed a pull-down ladder into our attic and installed some plywood floors. We now have about 1,000 square feet of storage space above our heads.

Neither of these solutions were *exactly* what we wanted (a new house) but they were little steps toward finding ways to live the life we want now. You can take this idea and easily apply it to all the sections of your dream board.

Freedom Number to Dream Number

Reaching your Freedom Number is an amazing feeling. It means your business is finally to the point where it can support your family's needs 100%! This is a huge accomplishment, and you should be proud of yourself.

But your work is not yet done. Remember back in Section 2, when we defined your Freedom number? We also introduced your Dream Number. *That* number is the one that allows you to reach all those items on your vision board—the number that gets you everything you and your family want in your life.

It's really easy to get comfortable at that Freedom Number. You're making enough to take care of your family. Maybe you've gotten your business to a good point and things feel simple and easy. Keep going! You started this thing for a reason. Remember that reason and keep forcing yourself to step out of your comfort zone so you can continue to grow your business and your life. As you continue to increase your income, use your roadmap to achieve the different items on your vision board, such as the bigger house, the Disney trip, deeper relationships, and the impact that you want to have on the world. Remember, the more money you make (after expenses), the more freedom you have and the more you can help others.

Section 6:
Stop Self Sabotage

Section Summary:

This book has provided you a step-by-step plan for how to build your ideal life, from figuring out what that is, to the steps required to build a business that will help make it a reality. If you trust the process, you can join the small but growing group of people who not only have big dreams but go after them and make them a reality. But even with a proven process to follow, you will find various roadblocks and barriers that will arise.

The goal of this section is to help you identify these barriers and navigate past them so you can put this place into action.

Why You Won't Follow Anything in This Book

We live in amazing times. The technological advancements that have occurred over the last several decades, and even the past 10 years, have been astonishing. The average person now has way more computing power in the smartphone in their pocket than we had when we first sent a space shuttle to the moon. These are truly remarkable times.

With this advancement of technology, we now have more access to information than ever before in the history. We can simply ask our phones a question and, within seconds, have the answer. So, you would think that with all of this information at our fingertips, more people would be happier with their lives and living the lifestyle that they desire. Yet this isn't the case. We are often seeing more examples of unhappiness, depression, unprecedented level of debt, and a high rate of divorces (according to the American Psychological Association). If we have all of the information that we need to be successful and happy, why aren't more people living happier and more successful lives?

The answer lies in the mirror. *It's you.*

You see, having all of the information in the world on how to be happy or successful won't work if you don't implement it. To move from *learning something* to *taking action on it* can be scary. It forces us to put forth effort, which means that it might take work, be difficult, and not work out the first time. It requires us to change, to be open to exploring who we are and the stories that we have in our heads about us and how the world works. It opens us up to failure. And it exposes us to the opinions and criticisms of others.

So often times people will have the desire to change, and they will take the first step. They will seek information, such as reading a book like this. They will get the knowledge, maybe even put a plan together, but then stop. They experience everything described above, they stop, and they don't ever get to live the life that they truly desire.

We had a great example of this happen as we were writing this book. We were right in the middle of a looming deadline but decided that we needed to take a break. We invited some friends over to hang out at our house. (Let's call them Sam and Alex.) Tom will take you through what transpired that night below.

After Sam and Alex spent some time playing with the kids, we finally got them into bed and could enjoy some adult time with our friends. Ariana and Alex left to hang out at a local bar and catch up. Meanwhile, myself and Sam hung out at the house and caught up on life/business over a few craft beers (as often happens). What unfolded was interesting, and a perfect example to illustrate this point. Before Ariana and Alex even left, I had the laptop out and was walking Sam through the book and the plans for it. What ensued was a deep discussion around this book— the format, the content, how the writing was going, the marketing plans, etc. For 45 minutes, I showed and explained the book to Sam. But Sam just wasn't getting it.

"What people want is something to implement right away and give them a quick win," Sam would say. "Nobody is going to read all of this, especially if they can't get a quick win from it. So *who* is the book for?"

I answered, "This book is for people who are seeking more freedom in our lives. So many of us know that we are capable of more, but we get stuck on the traditional path and aren't sure how to get off of it. This book shows them how to get clarity on what they want out of life and gives them a simple process to follow to build their business and make it a reality. It's typically focused on the entrepreneur, but the really cool thing is that all of these activities are designed to help entrepreneurial families get aligned and build the right business that they need to create the life that they crave."

I then showed Sam how we planned to continue helping people after they read the book. I showed them the additional content, templates and training that people could get after purchasing the book from our website. I showed him the process that hundreds of entrepreneurs have gone through as they had worked with us, which has allowed these entrepreneurs to truly reflect and get a clear view on what they wanted out of life, a roadmap to get their Freedom Number, the financial pieces that would be required, how to take their idea and make money, set up their business to be able to grow without taking over their lives, leave their jobs, and live their ideal life. In fact, that same process is the foundation of this book. This book came as a result of us implementing this process ourselves and with our clients, testing, getting feedback and refining over and over again. So, we know that it works.

Even with all of that, Sam wasn't seeing it. "That's all great Tom, but people need to be able to implement what they learn." So, then I showed them the templates that people could download, which would help them implement what they were learning in the book. "Yeah, but people don't need more templates. What they need is something like an activity to brainstorm all of their business ideas."

I was struggling. I was definitely open to feedback and wanted holes punched in the book concept so that we could close the gaps before getting it to the publisher, but this just wasn't adding up. Nearly all of the clients whom we worked with in the past said they came to us because of our ability to take a lot of disparate information, combine and simplify it, then create simple processes and templates to help them implement it. They also loved that we helped them build their business in support of their life, which is something that is rarely talked about in business books. Why was Sam not seeing that and seemingly going against everything that we thought we were doing right with the book?

"Oh, let me show you the third section of the book. It's called Concept to Cash, and the first activity is having people brainstorm with Post-It Notes on different businesses that they could potentially start."

"That's it!" said Sam. "You need to put that section first. Otherwise, no one is going to read through the first two boring sections that aren't even about business to make it to that point." Maybe it was a few of the beers kicking in, but I was starting to see Sam's point. If people didn't see the value in the first two sections, maybe they wouldn't make it to Section 3 and never create that life that they wanted. We needed to make sure that we resolved this issue.

I continued considering these thoughts through the rest of the night. After the girls returned and our friends left, we went to bed. Even though we both needed sleep, Ariana and I began talking about the night, as we often do. We each discussed of conversations that we had had during the night. I shared my conversation with Sam, and Ariana filled me in on her conversations with Alex. She said that Sam and Alex were struggling to pull everything together. Sam has a lot of different business ideas going on, but none of them are making very much money. Even so, he continues to spend money on new things. He just jumps into new ideas. Alex tried to continue to support him, but she feels like she is the only one who is thinking about their future. It took them a long time to get married, and so much of their lives seem to revolve around the business. She wants to be supportive, but it's like the rest of their lives have to be put on hold until one of these business ideas finally succeeds. And this keeps happening as Sam can't focus on one idea long enough to make it work. She's concerned that this will delay or even stop them from living the life that they want—like having kids, traveling, etc.

I recognized the path that Ariana was describing all too well. It was the trap that I initially fell into, and the trap we see so many entrepreneurs fall into. When Sam and I were talking, he wasn't seeing the value of the book until I showed him the third section, which was about business. He pretty much just wanted to skip the first two sections about life and money and get right to business, literally. He figured he could come back and focus on those *after* the business had success.

And that was it.

"Sam doesn't realize that HE needs to read this book!" Ariana shouted.

This book is exactly what Sam needs to hear. He needs to see that it isn't all about business, and that in addition to serving his customers, the business needs to serve *their lives*. But Sam was so caught up in trying to create a successful business that he was neglecting their lives and continuing down a slippery slope. The more he put into making the business work, the further apart Sam and Alex got. Maybe it wasn't visible on the surface, but each missed date night, every moment the business took time or money away from Sam and Alex's personal life was a withdrawal from their relationship bank. The basic concept of the relationship bank is that each relationship you have is like a bank account. Your balance starts at $0. Each positive interaction you have increases the balance, and each negative interaction withdraws money.

Without enough deposits (positive interactions), the bank account will draw down to $0, and even negative. When this happens, bad things occur. Relationships get strained. Spouses don't communicate as well and stop turning towards each other and start turning away. They don't know each other as well and drift further apart. Sometimes this goes on for years, and although they look happy on the outside, they are not. Sometimes it ends in divorce. Sometimes it ends in suicide. Regardless, it heads in a direction away from a happy and fulfilled life.

We've seen numerous businesses succeed, while marriages and lives have fallen apart at the same time. So, when entrepreneurs tell us they want to build the business first and will get back to their life and family once the business succeeds, we cringe. In many cases, there isn't a marriage to get back to. If it does survive, it is often damaged and requires a lot of work. In other cases, the business doesn't work *and* the marriage is left struggling.

We don't want this to happen, and it is our mission—not only with this book, but also with all the work that we do with entrepreneurs—to help couples who start businesses together learn how to integrate their businesses into their lives so they can be happy.

So, if you are reading this book as the entrepreneur, take a moment and answer this question honestly: *Are you Sam? Are you trying so hard to make your business work that you are letting other important areas of your life fall apart, potentially without even realizing it?* And don't just ask yourself this. We challenge you to go and ask your spouse. Ask your spouse how happy he or she is on a scale from 1 to 10. How does he or she feel about the business? Your relationship? Your happiness as a couple? And ask your spouse how he or she believes you can help improve it and support them.

If you are Alex, the non-entrepreneur, ask yourself the following questions: *Are you and Sam aligned on what's important? How do you really feel about the business, and does Sam know this? Are you and Sam aligned on what you want your future to look like, and are you making sure to incorporate elements of that into your life now, even as you work on making the business work?*

The process that we have laid out in this book is simple, but it is not easy. These words are often used interchangeably, and as a result, people often struggle when they mix them up.

Simple - Not complicated or containing complexity.

Easy - Achieved without great effort or difficulties.

Often a process is laid out in a simplistic way. For example, we have organized the process for building your ideal life and the business to support it in a simple way in this book. The major aspects are organized into various sections (and have sub-steps within each section). Simple. Trust the process. Don't overcomplicate it, try to change it or look for shortcuts.

But for you to take this process and implement it is not easy. It takes a significant amount of effort and growth to take what we have given you in this book and apply it to your situation to create the life that you desire. Your life is different from everyone around you. You have a different background and will face different challenges. You have different strengths and weaknesses. You have different stories that you tell yourself and limiting beliefs on what is possible. You may be aware of some of these, but there are likely many that you don't have awareness of yet. And even for the ones that you are aware of, you likely have pushed tackling some of them off because it won't be easy to address and work past them.

The Mistakes To Avoid

If you are still here, then there is hope! You've decided that you want to make this work. Here are a few more *gotchas* that could trip you up on this journey.

Looking for Shortcuts

We live in a time of instant gratification. You want things, and you want them now! This is similar to an experiment that we came across several years ago. A study was done testing the ability for children to delay gratification. In the study, the child was given a marshmallow. They were told if they didn't eat it, they would then get a second marshmallow. Some children ate the first marshmallow and ended up with one, while others waited and got two. They studied these children as they grew and found that the ones who could delay gratification were often more successful in life.

Much of why people get in trouble is not being able to delay gratification. This is shown when people go into massive debt to purchase something that they can't afford if they paid cash, but can "afford" by going into debt and spreading the payments across many years. These people often don't do as well financially because they pay more and fall into the golden handcuffs (more on that shortly). We don't want to you delay all gratification as we want you to enjoy life today, but it is important to not live too much for today that you negatively impact your future lifestyle tomorrow.

This same mentality comes in when people seek to start a business. They want everything to happen now, and often get discouraged when they don't see success right away. We see so many people that get discouraged because their business isn't seeing the success that the desire, only to find out that they've only been at it for a few months. It's not to say that you can't succeed quickly, but the majority don't. When you don't succeed as fast as you want, you begin looking for shortcuts.

Tom was guilty of this when we spent all that money on the real estate training. He thought that if he spent all that money, things would suddenly work. A lot of people end up looking for shortcuts to get them to success faster, and as a result, end up spending a lot of time and money on programs and people who promise them what they desire but don't deliver. A lot of the value is in the journey, and no matter how much a program or person promises to fast track you to the end, there are simply steps that you must go through. So be wary of shortcuts. Sometimes they can get you there faster, other times not. If the shortcut was really proven, then it would just be called *the way*.

Thinking You Can Do It Alone

With that said, this journey can be very challenging to go on alone, and we don't recommend it. You can benefit from support at every stage of your journey. Determine what type of support and guidance you need and seek out the people and support who provide you with that. Every stage of your journey will introduce new challenges, and often require more and different support. Asking for help doesn't mean that you are weak or less capable. On the contrary, it shows that you are strong and willing to be vulnerable to succeed.

When you seek support, it's important to find the right people and the right type. Seek out people who align with your core values. Often times these are people who are doing/have done what you want to do. They've been there, so they know what it feels like and can guide you through the tough times.

As we mentioned seeking shortcuts, be careful not to fall for slick marketing. Don't make emotional or on the spot decisions. If you didn't think you needed to buy something at the beginning of the day, then suddenly some catchy marketing convinced you that you did, don't act right away. Take time to think about the next step on your path. Be sure this investment is the *right* investment. If it isn't, delay it for now until it is the right time. Once you decide that it is the right type of investment, be sure to compare it to other options out there and make sure this specific investment is the best for you. When you are facing an investment decision to help you, take a few days to consider. If it still feels like the right move, go for it. Not all investments will work out as you planned, but they will all provide lessons learned.

Not Validating Your Business Model

As you saw in Section 3 (Concept to Cash), things rarely go according to plan. When you are starting a business, that upfront research and validation are critical to your success. Remember when we released that "30 Day to Launch" course and it failed miserably? It did so because we didn't validate the idea. We meet entrepreneurs every day who are struggling to make their business work. In just about every case, people have skipped over building the foundation of their business (including making sure their business model is solid), and skipped to the "fun" stuff, like designing your logo, building your website, and actually creating your product or offer.

The problem is, your business model is like a puzzle. Think of that Lean Canvas that we discussed earlier. Each of those nine boxes are pieces of the puzzle that need to be put together. If your business model is missing pieces, such as the solution section, then your business will struggle. You won't have a solution that solves a problem or that your ideal customer will pay for. Or maybe you are shoehorning pieces of another puzzle in, but they just don't fit. Perhaps your target marketing channel is through LinkedIn, but it's not where your customers are.

Don't skip validating your business model. In addition, when you do encounter challenges later on in the business, come back to your model and dive in to figure out the root cause of the issues. This will help you break through.

Not Getting Clear on What's Important to You (Instead of What Others Think)

The reason this book started out talking about you, your family, and your life is because you need to be clear on what *you* want, rather than what other people want, or what you think you should be doing to make other people happy. If you make decisions based on what others want you to do or what you think you should do based on their opinions, you will not be happy. That's why it is so important to get clear on what you and your family want, and work towards making that a reality.

The (False) Golden Handcuffs

Tom here. After I had set the goal for Ariana and I to retire by age 35—but before I spent the $7,500-plus for the "advanced" real estate training course—I learned one of the most valuable lessons to achieving financial freedom. This lesson came from an unexpected place.

It was the second of three days that I spent at this real estate investment training and we were sitting down to play this board game called Cashflow 101. This game was created by Robert Kiyosaki, author of *Rich Dad, Poor Dad*. (If you ask a group of entrepreneurs to list one book that influenced them, *Rich Dad, Poor Dad* is likely to come up on that list.) I came across *Rich Dad, Poor Dad* early in my entrepreneurial career. The book is basically about Robert's "two dads"; his biological dad (poor dad) and his friend's dad (rich dad) and how they shaped his views on money and wealth.

Some of these lessons are...

- The poor and middle-class work for money, while the rich have money work for them.
- It's not how much money you make, but rather how much money you keep.
- Rich people acquire assets. Poor and middle class acquire liabilities that they think are assets.

That last one was revolutionary for me. In my pursuit of retiring by age 35, I had read numerous personal finance books to educate myself on money. Throughout my reading, I had picked up the basic definition of both assets and liabilities:

253

- *Assets* were anything that held value and could be exchange for money. This meant that obviously cash was an asset, but also things that you owned like your house and your car.
- *Liabilities* were anything that you owed money on. So, credit card debt and student loan debt were liabilities.

This was also how the bank defined these terms.

One of the basics that most personal finance books discussed was purchasing your home. Many places said it would be most people's biggest asset in their lifetime. This made sense. I had always heard stories of someone's grandparents paying $20,000 for their house, which is now worth $200,000 many years later. But in *Rich Dad, Poor Dad*, Robert Kiyoaski offered a different way to approach and think about assets vs. liabilities:

- *Assets* are anything that put money into your pocket.
- *Liabilities* are anything that take money out of your pocket.

This is a simple shift, but it is *oh so powerful*. So, coming back to the Cashflow 101 game, there were two parts to it and, therefore, two levels of winning. Part I was called "The Rat Race." During this part of the game, the game board was a circle, not too dissimilar from a hamster wheel. To win this part of the game, you needed to get out of the rat race and onto the fast track. To do this, you needed your cash flow from everything (except your paycheck) to exceed your monthly expenses. At that point, you can leave your job because the cash flow from your businesses and investments allow you to cover your monthly expenses.

Part II was called "The Fast Track." During this part of the game, you stopped playing on the smaller hamster wheel and got promoted to play on a larger outer track. To win this part of the game, you need to either buy your dream or generate $50,000/month in cash flow. To do this, you either needed to land on your dream or continue investing in businesses to generate the required cash flow. To start the game, each player randomly draws a profession card. This card tells you your profession for the game, such as nurse, lawyer, secretary, etc. Each profession card also included a personal financial statement, including income, assets, expenses and liabilities.

As we were selecting cards, I was hoping for one of the high-paying jobs (clearly Kiyosaki's lesson on how much money you keep being more important than how much you make hadn't sunk in yet). As luck would have it, I drew the doctor card. I was ecstatic! This should be easy.

As other players drew their cards, I saw a mechanic, an engineer, a janitor, and a police officer. After drawing, we each filled out our personal financial statements based on our profession cards, reviewed the rules, and got started.

We weren't 20 minutes into the game when I heard one of the other players shout out "Yes! I'm out of the rat race!" I was shocked. I looked down and I wasn't even close. I needed to generate $13,200 in passive income to leave the rat race, and I was only sitting at a few thousand.

"How the heck did you get out of the rat race already? I'm not even close!" I continued. "What profession are you?"

"The janitor," he responded.

"How the heck does the janitor beat the doctor? How much cash flow do you have?" I asked.

"$1,825," he said.

"What? How do you only need $1,825 to achieve freedom? I need $13,200!"

"Well, I actually only need $1,600, but the extra $225 isn't bad."

And there I sat, dumbfounded.

"But I still don't understand. How can you only need $1,600 of cash flow to achieve freedom?"

"Well, I don't have a lot of expenses. My taxes are $280, rent is $200, car payment is $60, credit card payment is $60, retail payment is $50, and my other expenses are $300."

"How is your rent so low? Where can you possibly rent an apartment for only $200?"

"Well, maybe I am sharing a house with a few roommates. I did that in college and that was about what I paid each month."

"Well, my mortgage payment is more than your entire passive income: $1,900." I almost said it like I was proud. As I listened to myself say it, I was amazed at what I was doing. I was "bragging" about how big my mortgage payments were to someone who had just achieved financial freedom.

Let that sink in.

As I listened to myself, the light bulb came on. We can each decide when we achieve financial freedom, but most of us will let the short-term desires prevent us from achieving freedom. Clearly this doctor did not need a $1,900/month mortgage, but by choosing it, this person decided that a bigger house was more important to them than their freedom. This was the same for the $380 car payment and the $270 credit card payment.

Even though this is a game, it is scary as to how similar this thought process is to real life. Many people will spend their money to acquire Kiyosaki's version of liabilities, meaning things that take money out of your pocket every month. This may start out simple, buying a couple of things that you want. Then you get a raise, and suddenly you tell yourself that you've worked hard to get that raise and deserve to reward yourself, so you buy more things. As time goes on, you end up building a prison around yourself, except it doesn't look like a prison. It looks like a nice house, a nice car, nice clothing, vacations, etc. It looks like you've made it!

The only problem is, you look like the doctor. You have a lot of nice stuff, but in the process, you've raised your Freedom Number so high that you need to make a lot of money in order to just cover your monthly expenses. This requires you to work harder and longer to keep up with the lifestyle and expenses that you've developed. Instead of your hard work freeing you, it has now created a prison. You want freedom, but now all of that stuff—and its associated monthly cost—keeps you from pursuing the freedom that you desire.

This is what is commonly known as the "golden handcuffs": When you make "good money" and need to make that to cover your expenses, but now you want to leave/do something different and you can't because your expenses are too high. You *need* the money, so you feel stuck. People get stuck here all the time. From the outside, they don't get sympathy, and are in fact often praised for the amazing lifestyle that they seem to have, even though they are miserable on the inside.

If this is you, keep reading. This prison isn't real; it's self-imposed. You did this to yourself. You bought those things. You created this lifestyle. In the process, you increased your expenses. As tough as this is to hear, there is also an amazing silver lining; because you created this prison and these are your handcuffs, that also means that you have the key to unlocking yourself. The key is to reduce your Freedom Number.

Tony Robbins, author, entrepreneur, philanthropist and life coach, has a great formula for happiness:

"Whenever you are happy with something in your life,
it is because right now, the conditions of your life match your blueprint,
or your belief about how life should be in that particular area."

So, if you are happy, then your current life conditions equal how you believe that your life should be. If you are not happy, then you can either change how you believe your life should be, or your current life conditions.

Going back to the first section of this book and the Life Planner that you filled out, you identified what you wanted out of life and a path to get there. If that is still accurate, then you need to change your current conditions to get you there. Take some time to look at everything in your life. Take a look at what each thing is costing you, in terms of time, money and energy, as well as how they are benefiting you. For the things that are costing you more than they are benefiting, begin brainstorming a change that you can make to switch that around. For example, if your mortgage payment is costing you more than it is benefiting you—because you are working all the time and can't enjoy your house—look to sell it and get a smaller house. You may like your car, but the monthly loan payment *plus* high insurance *plus* maintenance may be costing you more than it is benefiting you.

When you look at all aspects of your life and start eliminating and reducing costs, you begin having less complexity and strain in your life. You also begin increasing your awareness and clarity on what moves you towards your goals and what is holding you back. With the increased awareness and clarity, many people find that the reason they got off course and are unhappy is because they were living how they *thought* society and other people wanted them to live, instead of how *they* want to live. That's why taking the time to go through and fill out the questions on the Life Planner is so important. This clarity will allow you to begin taking action and making changes to get you the life that you desire. You can take the handcuffs off, leave the prison behind and start living the life that you truly want, on your terms.

Chapter 6.4

Your Next Steps

You've made it! That was a lot to get through, we know. We poured more than a decade of education and experience on you. Our goal was to provide a simple roadmap and actionable items that will allow you to move forward in achieving financial freedom and living your ideal life. Hopefully we've accomplished our mission.

We would love to hear from you on your insights, takeaways and questions. You can do this by leaving us an honest review of the book on our website (or the bookseller's website). Additionally, you can also send us an e-mail at <u>hello@</u> <u>tomandariana.com</u>.

We've put together a companion to this book to help you on this journey, which is the Lifestyle Builders Starter Pack. It contains templates, guides, and other resources to help you get the most out of this book. You can get this for free by going to <u>www.lifestylebuildersbook.com</u>.

If you'd like to continue to dive deeper into topic discussed in this book, be sure to subscribe to the Lifestyle Builders Podcast on your favorite podcast player or by visiting <u>www.lifestylebuilderspodcast.com</u>.

And finally, we want to leave you with this. No matter where you are at in your life, it's never too late to make a change and go after your dreams. The systems and processes that we've outlined in this book work. We've done it. Others have done it. Now it's your time to do it.

Become a Lifestyle Builder.
Create Your Business.
Quit Your Job.
And Live Your Ideal Life.

Acknowledgements

Writing this book together was one of the hardest things we have attempted to date. If not for the immense support and cheering on from all of you, who knows what would have happened! No amount of thanks can convey the gratitude we feel, but we'll try.

To all of our parents, for always believing in us and going along with our crazy ideas. To standing by for the ups and downs and taking care of us when we needed help. And to the "Grandma Musketeers" for watching the kids on every conference trip, planning birthday parties, and making weekly visits.

To the rest of our family and all of our friends, for understanding why we couldn't make every get together, and for loving us anyways. And for supporting us through all the business and life evolutions for the last 10+ years. A special shout-out to Brianna, Steph & Lizzie, for keeping me (Ariana) sane! Thank you for all the "girls" nights.

To our beautiful children, Elena and Ty. You may not understand it now, but someday we hope you'll look back on this time and appreciate the blood sweat and tears we put in to give you an amazing and fulfilled life with us.

To the man who made this all possible, who inspired us to share this message far and wide, Dan Miller. You and Joanne are who we want to be when we "grow up"! And for introducing us into the Morgan James Family. To Chris & Jim for believing in our book, and to our team at Morgan James Publishing for helping us to make it come alive!

To our awesomesauce editor, Brian Klems, for sticking by us and this project during everything you went through. For giving us spectacular feedback and suggestions that made this book even better, especially the ones that had us laughing. And to Brandi Johnson for making the connection! To our rock star image designer, Sarah Guilliot, for capturing the visuals and making them come alive. To Blossom Fox and Heather Clark for helping us keep it all together behind the scenes, during the chaos of life, book & business.

To all of our Lifestyle Builders, for bearing with us as we built out this framework, and for putting in the work even when it was hard. You are our first inspiration and your everyday wins are what keep us going.

To our Entrepreneur friends (many of you who have become more like family) – Jaclyn & Chris Mellone, Jason & Audrey Brown, Rachel & Poul Pedersen, Christine McAlister, Christi Bender, Heather Gray, Jessica Lorimer, Dorothea Bolzicolona Volpe, Nadja Williamson, Kay Fabella, April Dryden Beach, Amanda Bond, Dale Hensel, Arne Giske, Dustin Heiner, Armando & Christian Cruz, Mike & Katie Young, Nicole Vosburgh …. And to all of the communities we've become a part of: the #Scroupies, the FinCon family, Amy's B-School crew, the Power Couples Community, of course Ariana's local Rochester Boss Moms!

To all of you who have helped spark our vision over the years – Shane & Jocelyn Sams, Jill & Josh Stanton, Alex & Cadey Charfen, Mike Michalowitz, John Lee Dumas & Kate Erickson, Pat Flynn, Amy Porterfield, Chris Hogan, Dave Ramsey & the rest of the Ramsey Team, David Bach, Alexi Panos & Preston Smiles, Chris Winfield.

To Despina, for keeping us stable! Your guidance has helped us to both build a stronger marriage, and to strengthen us as individuals as well. Our life is a much happier & healthier one, thanks to you.

And to all of you readers, for being our inspiration to write this book! Thank you all for coming on this journey with us, and for being unapologetic about going after your best life.

About the Authors

Tom & Ariana Sylvester are Lifestyle Builders, entrepreneurs and business consultants. With three thriving (and very different) businesses of their own, Tom & Ariana each bringing a variety of experience & knowledge. The couple graduated from SUNY Oswego together in 2006—Tom with a bachelor's in computer science and Ariana with a bachelor's in Zoology—and were married in 2008.

Tom continued his love of learning and business with a master's in management in 2012 from Nazareth University. He then went on to expand his experience in the corporate world consulting with Fortune 500 executives and their teams, and uses the wealth of knowledge gained there to continue helping entrepreneurs around the globe.

Ariana grew her experience by subsequently managing the day-to-day of each of their businesses: a real estate company, a retail wine & liquor store, and the business coaching company, while also raising their 2 kids. (You can find more of their story at TomandAriana.com)

The couple resides with their children and pets in Rochester, NY, where you can find Tom playing video games in their home theater and Ariana watching re-runs of *The Big Bang Theory*…Bazinga.

Endnotes

1   Office Tally. 2006. Dunder Mifflin mission statement. [https://www. officetally.com/dunder-mifflin-mission-statement] Accessed January 2019.

2   Locke, Tim. 2015. Drink Water Before Meals to Lose Weight? [https:// www.webmd.com/diet/obesity/news/20150828/water-weight-meals-obesity] Accessed September 2018.

3   Wolan, Christian. 2011. The Real Story of Twitter. [https://www.forbes. com/sites/christianwolan/2011/04/14/the-real-story-of-twitter/#3f-5ca38366af] Accessed October 2018.

4   3M. 2018. From Humble Beginnings to Fortune 500. [https://www.3m. com/3M/en_US/company-us/about-3m/history/] Accessed November 2018.

5   Maurya, Ash. 2012. Why Lean Canvas vs Business Model Canvas? [https://blog.leanstack.com/why-lean-canvas-vs-business-model-canvas-af-62c0f250f0] Accessed May 2018.

6   Kailath, Ryan & Selyuhk, Alina. 2018. Apple Becomes World's 1st Private-Sector Company Worth $1 Trillion [https://www.npr. org/2018/08/02/632697978/apple-becomes-worlds-1st-private-sector-com-pany-worth-1-trillion] Accessed January 2019.

7   Lencioni, Patrick. 2010. Getting Naked: A Business Fable About Shedding The Three Fears That Sabotage Client Loyalty. Jossey-Bass, California. 240pp.

8   The Table Group. 2013. The Glossary of Key Terms. [https://www.table-group.com/imo/media/doc/The%20Glossary%20of%20Key%20Terms.pdf] Accessed September 2018.

Printed in the USA
CPSIA information can be obtained
at www.ICGtesting.com
JSHW022214140824
68134JS00018B/1053